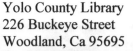

PREHISTORIC EARTH

LAST OF THE DINOSAURS

THE CRETACEOUS PERIOD

THE PREHISTORIC EARTH

THE PREHISTORIC EARTH

LAST OF THE DINOSAURS

THE CRETACEOUS PERIOD

Thom Holmes

CHELSEA HOUSE
PUBLISHERS
An imprint of Infobase Publishing

THE PREHISTORIC EARTH: Last of the Dinosaurs

Chelsea House
An imprint of Infobase Publishing
132 West 31st Street
New York NY 10001

Library of Congress Cataloging-in-Publication Data

Holmes, Thom.
  Last of the dinosaurs : the Cretaceous period / Thom Holmes.
     p. cm. — (The prehistoric Earth)
  Includes bibliographical references and index.
  ISBN 978-0-8160-5962-1 (hardcover)
  1. Dinosaurs. 2. Paleontology—Cretaceous. I. Title.
  QE861.4.H653 2009
  567.9—dc22   2008038331

Chelsea House books are available at special discounts when purchased in bulk quantities for businesses, associations, institutions, or sales promotions. Please call our Special Sales Department in New York at (212) 967-8800 or (800) 322-8755.

You can find Chelsea House on the World Wide Web at http://www.chelseahouse.com

Text design by Kerry Casey
Cover design by Salvatore Luongo
Section opener images © John Sibbick

Printed in the United States of America

Bang NMSG 10 9 8 7 6 5 4 3 2 1

This book is printed on acid-free paper.

All links and Web addresses were checked and verified to be correct at the time of publication. Because of the dynamic nature of the Web, some addresses and links may have changed since publication and may no longer be valid.

Contents

PREFACE

To be curious about the future one must know something about the past.

Humans have been recording events in the world around them for about 5,300 years. That is how long it has been since the Sumerian people, in a land that is today part of southern Iraq, invented the first known written language. Writing allowed people to document what they saw happening around them. The written word gave a new permanency to life. Language, and writing in particular, made history possible.

History is a marvelous human invention, but how do people know about things that happened before language existed? Or before humans existed? Events that took place before human record keeping began are called *prehistory*. Prehistoric life is, by its definition, any life that existed before human beings existed and were able to record for posterity what was happening in the world around them.

Prehistory is as much a product of the human mind as history. Scientists who specialize in unraveling clues of prehistoric life are called *paleontologists*. They study life that existed before human history, often hundreds of thousands and millions, and even billions, of years in the past. Their primary clues come from fossils of animals, plants, and other organisms, as well as geologic evidence about the Earth's topography and climate. Through the skilled and often clever interpretation of fossils, paleontologists are able to reconstruct the appearances, lifestyles, environments, and relationships of ancient life-forms. While paleontology is grounded in a study of prehistoric life, it draws on many other sciences to complete an accurate picture of the past. Information from the fields of biology, zoology, geology, chemistry, meteorology, and even astrophysics is called into play to help the paleontologist view the past through the lens of today's knowledge.

If a writer were to write a history of all sports, would it be enough to write only about table tennis? Certainly not. On the shelves of bookstores and libraries, however, we find just such a slanted perspective toward the story of the dinosaurs. Dinosaurs have captured our imagination at the expense of many other equally fascinating, terrifying, and unusual creatures. Dinosaurs were not alone in the pantheon of prehistoric life, but it is rare to find a book that also mentions the many other kinds of life that came before and after the dinosaurs.

The Prehistoric Earth is a series that explores the evolution of life from its earliest forms 3.5 billion years ago until the emergence of modern humans some 300,000 years ago. Four volumes in the series trace the story of the dinosaurs. Six other volumes are devoted to the kinds of animals that evolved before, during, and after the reign of the dinosaurs. *The Prehistoric Earth* covers the early explosion of life in the oceans; the invasion of the land by the first land animals; the rise of fishes, amphibians, reptiles, mammals, and birds; and the emergence of modern humans.

The Prehistoric Earth series is written for readers in middle school and high school. Based on the latest scientific findings in paleontology, *The Prehistoric Earth* is the most comprehensive and up-to-date series of its kind for this age group.

The first volume in the series, *Early Life*, offers foundational information about geologic time, Earth science, fossils, the classification of organisms, and evolution. This volume also begins the chronological exploration of fossil life that explodes with the incredible life-forms of Precambrian time and the Cambrian Period, more than 500 million years ago.

The remaining nine volumes in the series can be read chronologically. Each volume covers a specific geologic time period and describes the major forms of life that lived at that time. The books also trace the geologic forces and climate changes that affected the evolution of life through the ages. Readers of *The Prehistoric Earth* will see the whole picture of prehistoric life take shape. They will learn about forces that affect life on Earth, the directions that life can sometimes take, and ways in which all life-forms depend on each other in the environment. Along the way, readers also will meet many of the scientists who have made remarkable discoveries about the prehistoric Earth.

The language of science is used throughout this series, with ample definition and with an extensive glossary provided in each volume. Important concepts involving geology, evolution, and the lives of early animals are presented logically, step by step. Illustrations, photographs, tables, and maps reinforce and enhance the books' presentation of the story of prehistoric life.

While telling the story of prehistoric life, the author hopes that many readers will be sufficiently intrigued to continue studies on their own. For this purpose, throughout each volume, special "Think About It" sidebars offer additional insights or interesting exercises for readers who wish to explore certain topics. Each book in the series also provides a chapter-by-chapter bibliography of books, journals, and Web sites.

Only about one-tenth of 1 percent of all species of prehistoric animals are known from fossils. A multitude of discoveries remain to be made in the field of paleontology. It is with earnest, best wishes that I hope that some of these discoveries will be made by readers inspired by this series.

—Thom Holmes
Jersey City, New Jersey

ACKNOWLEDGMENTS

I want to thank the many dedicated and hardworking people at Chelsea House and Facts on File, some of whom I know but many of whom work behind the scenes. A special debt of gratitude goes to my editors—Frank Darmstadt, Brian Belval, Justine Ciovacco, Lisa Rand, and Shirley White—for their support and guidance in conceiving and making *The Prehistoric Earth* a reality. Frank and Brian were instrumental in fine-tuning the features of the series as well as accepting my ambitious plan for creating a comprehensive reference for students. Brian greatly influenced input during production. Shirley's excellent questions about the science behind the books contributed greatly to the readability of the result. The excellent copyediting of Mary Ellen Kelly was both thoughtful and vital to shaping the final manuscript. I thank Mary Ellen for her patience as well as her valuable review and suggestions that help make the books a success.

The most important collaborators on a series like this are the scientific consultants who lend their time to fact-check and advise the author. I am privileged to work with some of the brightest minds in paleontology on this series. Dr. Matthew Lamanna, assistant curator of vertebrate paleontology at the Carnegie Museum of Natural History, reviewed the draft of *Last of the Dinosaurs* and made many important suggestions that affected the course of the work. Matt also wrote the Foreword for the volume. Perhaps most importantly, Matt's own research on Cretaceous vertebrate faunas and fieldwork on several continents lends an extraordinary authenticity to the story of past life told in these pages.

Breathing life into prehistoric creatures is also the work of natural history artists, many of whom have contributed to this series. I especially want to thank John Sibbick, a major contributor to the artwork seen in *The Prehistoric Earth*. John's work is renowned among paleontologists, many of whom he has worked with side by side.

I want to thank Ben Creisler, whose "Dinosaur Translation and Pronunciation Guide" is my final word for the English translation of Greek, Latin, and other non-English taxonomic names used in this book. Ben's resource represents years of dedication to the somewhat cryptic but important task of understanding the meanings behind the scientific names of extinct animals.

In many ways, a set of books such as this requires years of preparation. Some of the work is educational, and I owe much gratitude to Dr. Peter Dodson of the University of Pennsylvania for his gracious and inspiring tutelage over the years. I also thank Dr. William B. Gallagher of the New Jersey State Museum for lessons learned both in the classroom and in the historic fossil beds of New Jersey. Another dimension of preparation requires experience digging fossils, and for giving me these opportunities I thank my friends and colleagues who have taken me into the field with them, including Phil Currie, Rodolfo Coria, Matthew Lammana, Josh Smith, and Rubén Martínez.

Finally comes the work needed to put thoughts down on paper and complete the draft of a book, a process that always takes many more hours than I plan on. I thank Anne for bearing with my constant state of busy-ness, jokes about jawless fishes, and penguin notes, and for helping me remember the important things in life. You are an inspiration to me. I also thank my daughter, Shaina, the true genius in the family and another constant inspiration, for always being supportive and humoring her dad's obsession with prehistoric life, even as he becomes part of it.

FOREWORD

To me, the Cretaceous Period is far and away the most interesting time in Earth history. In many ways, the Cretaceous can be thought of as the time when our planet grew up, or at least reached the condition it is in today. This process of "maturation" occurred on at least two main fronts: one involving the physical shape of the world, and the other regarding the organisms that inhabited it.

As readers of *The Prehistoric Earth* will recall from previous volumes, when the curtain lifted on the Mesozoic Era about 250 million years ago, all of the world's major landmasses were united as one gigantic supercontinent: Pangaea. As the Mesozoic wore on, and the Triassic Period passed into the Jurassic, the continents composing Pangaea began their tumultuous breakup. First, the northern continents, as the smaller but still enormous landmass of Laurasia, rifted from their southern counterparts, collectively known as Gondwana. During the Cretaceous, Laurasia and Gondwana themselves were torn to pieces by irresistible geologic forces, and by the end of this period, most of the continents we know today had come into existence.

This profound planetary facelift had far-reaching effects on the evolution of life. In the Cretaceous, land-living flora and fauna that had once spread throughout Pangaea now found themselves separated by seawater. As landmasses drifted inexorably apart, so too did the genetic makeup of organisms inhabiting them. Legions of new species appeared, and others vanished forever, with each of the newborn continents characterized by its own unique pattern of evolution and extinction. Approaching the end of the Cretaceous, every major landmass hosted plants and animals found nowhere else in the world.

Many of these evolutionary newcomers would have looked familiar to human eyes. By the middle stages of the Cretaceous, modern-style birds had taken wing, while the earliest-known snakes had slithered across land and even swum the seas. The first marsupials and placentals, the ancestors of all but five of the mammal species alive today, had invaded the world's forests and prairies. Perhaps the most consequential changes to environments around the globe, however, were driven by the Early Cretaceous origin of today's most dominant group of plants—the angiosperms, or flowering plants. The rise of flowers spurred innumerable changes to ecosystems worldwide. As these fast-growing, nutritious plants spread across the land, novel types of animals evolved to feast on them.

Multitudes of new non-avian dinosaurs evolved during the Cretaceous as well. Whereas Triassic and Jurassic dinosaurs were basically the same all around the world, Cretaceous dinosaurs, isolated by continental fragmentation, evolved along widely varying pathways in disparate areas of the globe. North America and Asia hosted many of the best-known and most recognizable dinosaur groups—tyrannosaurs, "raptors," duckbills, and horned and bone-headed dinosaurs, to name a few. Moreover, exciting new research on the southern landmasses, especially South America, Africa, Australia, and Madagascar, is revealing the equally spectacular and often bizarre dinosaurs that inhabited these areas as well. The majority of Southern Hemisphere dinosaurs are fundamentally distinct from their distant cousins in the northern continents. Imagine bulldog-faced carnivores with horned heads and ridiculously short arms, tall-spined fish-eaters with the skulls of crocodiles, and titanic, long-necked herbivores that include the largest land animals that have ever existed.

It was in search of these singular southern dinosaurs that I first came to know Thom Holmes. In 2000, Thom joined a paleontological expedition to Late Cretaceous rocks in southern Chubut Province, Argentina, led by my Patagonian colleague Rubén Martínez and me. Thom impressed us with his talent for finding fossils, his skill with a Frisbee, and most importantly, his curiosity and knowledge of natural history. Readers of *The Prehistoric Earth* are in good hands—Thom Holmes is an excellent and reliable guide to the prehistoric past.

In this ambitious book, Thom leads us on a tour of the Cretaceous world and the life-forms that called it home. Section One provides an overview of Cretaceous geography and climate, and chronicles the dawn of flowering plants. Sections Two and Three compose a "who's who" of Cretaceous dinosaurs that focuses not only on well-known Northern Hemisphere species but also on their distant Gondwanan relations. Section Four discusses the myriad nondinosaurian reptiles that thrived in Mesozoic oceans and skies, while the Conclusion introduces the cataclysmic end-Cretaceous extinction that wiped out all dinosaurs except birds.

So, without further delay, I invite you to begin your journey through the Cretaceous Period. I suspect that, after you've finished *Last of the Dinosaurs*, you'll agree that the Cretaceous was a critical time in the evolution of our world. Perhaps you'll even want to join me in seeking answers to its mysteries.

—Dr. Matt Lamanna
Carnegie Museum of Natural History
Pittsburgh, Pennsylvania

INTRODUCTION

The story of the **evolution** of the dinosaurs, the first two episodes of which are described in the companion volumes *Dawn of the Dinosaur Age* and *Time of the Giants*, concludes in *Last of the Dinosaurs*. The conclusion of the dinosaur story introduces the largest land **predators** that ever existed, explores the dinosaurian response to the rise of flowering plants, and introduces the fifth and last of the great orders of **extant** vertebrates: the birds.

The story continues by investigating the dinosaurs that arose during the Early and Late Cretaceous Epochs, a span of 80 million years that makes up nearly half of the total Age of Dinosaurs. This important span saw the dinosaur world divided by continental shifts that created clearly distinct separations between the Northern and Southern Hemispheres—a geologic effect that also isolated some dinosaur **clades**, resulting in divergent evolutionary trends. The giant sauropods (**Sauropoda**) continued to flourish in the southern continents but were widely displaced in some regions north of the equator by a clade of plant eaters that were better adapted to eating flowering plants: the iguanodonts and hadrosaurs. Another dramatic transition took place in the evolution of some small predatory dinosaurs, many of which sported feathers and whose **forelimbs** gradually transformed into wings, launching the rise of birds. Other key dinosaurian players reached their pinnacle of diversity during the dinosaurs' final act, including the diverse and successful horned dinosaurs and bone-headed dinosaurs.

Dinosaurs were not alone in their world, so *Last of the Dinosaurs* explores other important extinct Mesozoic reptiles. These include the masters of the sky known as the pterosaurs (flying reptiles) and a variety of plentiful oceangoing marine reptiles such as the ichthyosaurs, plesiosaurs, marine crocodiles, and others. *Last of the*

Dinosaurs must necessarily conclude with the catastrophic **mass extinction** that wiped out many of the headliners of the Mesozoic, thereby clearing the stage and making room for the age's understudies—the birds and the mammals—to diversify and dominate after the time of the dinosaurs.

OVERVIEW OF *LAST OF THE DINOSAURS*

Last of the Dinosaurs begins by looking at the geological and ecological conditions that created opportunities for the expansion of dinosaurs of the Early and Late Cretaceous Epochs. Section One encompasses worldwide geologic and climatic changes of the Cretaceous **Period**. Chapter 1 describes widespread changes to ocean and land environments, including changes to climates worldwide, that served as catalysts for the radiation of dinosaurs and other vertebrates. Temperate global climates allowed dinosaurs to live in every part of their world. The rise of flowering plants was the cause of dramatic turnover in the food supply of these animals and also affected their continued success and survival.

Section Two encompasses the evolution of saurischian dinosaurs of the Cretaceous Period. Chapter 2 describes the continuing evolution of the sauropods and the last of their line. It was during this time that the radiation of these animals shifted to the southern continents and resulted in the appearance of the biggest sauropods of all. Chapter 3 revisits the theropods, exploring several parallel lines of evolution that led, at one end, to the largest land predators of all time and, at the other, to the small predatory dinosaurs that were the ancestors of birds.

The origin of birds is explored in Chapter 4; the chapter introduces the probable roots of their evolution and reveals some of the controversies surrounding the link between dinosaurs and birds. Within this context, the spectacular Early Cretaceous **fossil** beds of China are introduced; these beds are the source of many specimens of feathered, nonflying dinosaurs and early bird specimens that have greatly aided the study of bird origins.

Section Three encompasses the evolution of ornithischian dinosaurs of the Cretaceous Period, including several groups that appeared for the first time during this span. Chapter 5 introduces the herbivorous ornithopods, whose subgroups include the basal iguanodonts and hadrosaurs, many with astonishingly varied head crests and dental **adaptations**. Chapter 6 describes two additional clades of widespread and varied plant-eating dinosaurs: the Ceratopsia, or horned dinosaurs, and the Pachycephalosauria, or bone-headed dinosaurs.

Section Four encompasses the nondinosaurian reptiles of the Mesozoic Era. Chapter 7 introduces the flying reptiles known as the Pterosauria, a successful and varied clade of animals representing the first vertebrates to have developed powered flight. Pterosaurs lived in the world of the dinosaurs as masters of the skies. Chapter 8 describes a variety of extinct marine reptiles that dominated the oceans of the Mesozoic. These creatures had a worldwide distribution and included the dolphinlike ichthyosaurs; the walruslike placodonts; long- and short-necked nothosaurs, plesiosaurs, and pliosaurs; the monstrous mosasaurs; extinct marine crocodiles; and the first marine turtles.

The conclusion of *Last of the Dinosaurs* explores the mass extinction that ended the reign of the **non-avian** dinosaurs and many other terrestrial and marine creatures of the time, and provides a framework for assessing what might have happened to cause such a catastrophic disappearance of life.

Each chapter uses an abundance of tables, figures, and photos to depict the life, habitats, and changing evolutionary patterns affecting the evolution of the vertebrates. Several chapters also include "Think About It" sidebars that elaborate on interesting issues, people, history, and discoveries related to Mesozoic life.

Last of the Dinosaurs builds on foundational principles of geology, fossils, and the study of life that are introduced in other volumes of this series, *The Prehistoric Earth*. Readers who would like to refresh their knowledge of certain basic terms and principles in the study of past life may want to consult the glossary in the back of *Last of the Dinosaurs*. Perhaps most important to keep in mind are the basic rules governing evolution: that the process of evolution is set in motion first by the traits inherited by individuals and then by the interaction of a population of a **species** with its habitat. Changes that enable the population to survive accumulate generation after generation, often producing and allowing species to adapt to changing conditions in the world around them. As Charles Darwin (1809–1882) explained, "The small differences distinguishing varieties of the same species steadily tend to increase, till they equal the greater differences between species of the same **genus**, or even of distinct genera." These are the rules of nature that served to stoke the engine of evolution throughout Earth's history, ultimately giving rise to the myriad forms of life whose descendants still populate Earth.

SECTION ONE:
THE WORLD OF
THE DINOSAURS

1

THE EARLY AND LATE CRETACEOUS EPOCHS

The Cretaceous Period, which spanned 80 million years, was the last great time span of the Mesozoic Era. Coming to a crashing climax 65.5 million years ago, it marked the last reign of the dinosaurs and their reptilian cousins in the oceans and in the air. The name *Cretaceous* is Latin for "chalk" and refers to the abundant layers of chalk deposits that are found in **sedimentary** rocks of Europe that date from this period. The Cretaceous Period is further subdivided into two epochs: the Early Cretaceous (145 million to 100 million years ago) and the Late Cretaceous (100 million to 65.5 million years ago). The accompanying table summarizes the major time divisions of the Mesozoic Era, including the Cretaceous Period, and important milestones in the evolution of life.

SHAPING THE WORLD OF THE DINOSAURS

Whereas the Jurassic Period was relatively quiet geologically, the geography of the Cretaceous Period witnessed a dramatic resurgence of tectonic plate movements. **Continental drift** during the Cretaceous Period caused the continued breakup of the northern and southern supercontinents of **Laurasia** and **Gondwana**, separating them into landmasses approximating their present-day configuration. The northern Laurasia included areas that became North America, Europe, and Asia. The southern landmass of Gondwana included the regions now known as South America, Africa, India, Madagascar, Australia, and Antarctica. During the Cretaceous, the Atlantic Ocean spread open, submerging the land bridges that once

EVOLUTIONARY MILESTONES OF THE MESOZOIC ERA

Epoch	Span (millions of years ago)	Duration (millions of years)	Organismal Milestones
Early Triassic	251–245	6	Diversification and dispersal of amniotes, particularly synapsids and diapsids
Middle Triassic	245–228	17	Rise of pterosaurs and sauropterygian marine reptiles
Late Triassic	228–200	28	Earliest frogs, turtles, crocodylians, dinosaurs, and mammals Diversification of conifers
Mass extinction			Casualties: most nonmammalian synapsids, phytosaurs, placodonts, nothosaurs
Early Jurassic	200–175.6	24	Radiation of carnivorous and herbivorous dinosaurs, first crocodilians
Middle Jurassic	175.6–161	15	Rise of armored, plated, and ornithopod dinosaurs, diversification of sauropods
Late Jurassic	161–145.5	16	Dominance of sauropods, diversification of theropods, first birds and horned dinosaurs
Early Cretaceous	145.5–100	46	Continued diversification of dinosaurs, birds, marine reptiles (other than ichthyosaurs, which were already becoming extinct), and pterosaurs First marsupial and placental mammals Rise of angiosperms—the flowering plants
Late Cretaceous	100–65.5	34	Largest known theropods and sauropods, diversification of horned dinosaurs, appearance and radiation of hadrosaurs, snakes, mosasaurs, and modern-style birds,
Mass extinction			Casualties: Non-avian dinosaurs, opposite birds, pterosaurs, ammonites, all marine reptiles except turtles

connected North America with Europe and South America with Africa. India broke from Gondwana and began its northerly drift toward Asia. North America was divided by a vast inland sea that, at its greatest extent, dissected the continent from the northwest Arctic to the Gulf of Mexico.

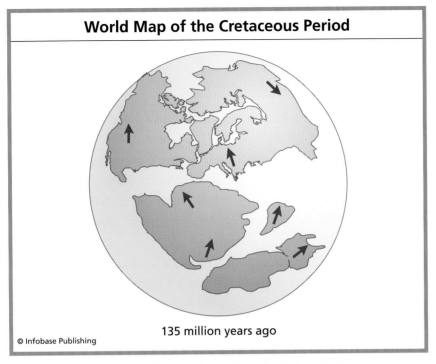

World Map of the Cretaceous Period

135 million years ago

© Infobase Publishing

The geologic positioning of the major continents during the Cretaceous Period

The northwest coast and southern tip of South America were largely under water. North Africa was largely under water, as was the northern edge of India. Much of Great Britain and the northern half of Africa were under water as well, as was much of southern Europe and northeastern Australia. High water levels reached their peak during the middle of the Cretaceous, about 100 million years ago, when about one-third of the present land area of Earth was submerged. This dramatic rise in sea level was caused by an acceleration of seafloor spreading that enlarged ocean ridges, formed undersea mountains, and displaced water to areas that once were dry land. Such seafloor spreading also spurred the continued breakup of the continents. The rise of the oceans was also affected by the melting of polar ice caps because of the greenhouse climate of the middle Cretaceous. By the end of the Cretaceous, a general slowdown in tectonic activity took place, reducing the size of ocean ridges and underwater mountains and forming deeper ocean basins that allowed continents to shed some of the water that had overflowed onto them.

CLIMATES AND HABITATS

The Middle and Late Jurassic Epochs were evenly warm and temperate across much of the globe. This is not to say that the world had only one uniform climate during the Jurassic. Just like today, there were Jurassic deserts, Jurassic mountains, Jurassic islands, and other regions, each of them with their own unique climatic regimes. Although the poles were warmer than they are at present, they were still cooler than equatorial regions.

The submergence of large portions of continental landmasses during the Cretaceous Period continued a trend towards uniformly warm temperatures and profoundly affected worldwide climates. This was largely because of having so much more of the Earth covered with ocean in the preceding epochs. Because solar radiation is readily absorbed by the sea, the warming of Cretaceous oceans and the air above them was great enough to spread warming winds over the continents. There were no ice caps; fossil evidence of plants and animals across the continents, from pole to pole, strongly suggests that subtropical climates had reached well into the interiors of continents of both the Northern and Southern Hemispheres.

The first part of the Cretaceous was the coolest time in the period; the middle Cretaceous was the warmest, and the Late Cretaceous was in between. Fossils show that plants such as sequoia and magnolia trees, which cannot survive freezing temperatures, were living in Greenland during the middle of the Cretaceous Period, a testament to that island's once mild but northerly climate. Evidence of dinosaurs in the form of **trackways** and body fossils has been found repeatedly in some of the coldest regions of today's planet, including the Antarctic, Alaska, and northern Asia. Dinosaurs were alive and well in the northern and southern polar regions of Earth during the Cretaceous, a testament to the rising warmth of the planet during the first part of the Cretaceous.

A rise in Cretaceous sea levels also corresponded with increased periods of sedimentation and the formation of fossils from this period. Exposures of Cretaceous sedimentary rocks are widespread across the surface of the Earth, the result being that about half of the known dinosaurs have emerged from rocks of Cretaceous age.

THE RISE OF FLOWERING PLANTS

Until the Early Cretaceous Epoch, the world's **flora** was dominated by ferns and **gymnosperms**—seed plants whose seed embryos are not protected by a fruit, cone, or other body. Gymnosperms first appeared in the late Paleozoic Era and became dominant during the first half of the Mesozoic Era. They are still represented today by more than 600 known species of conifers (evergreen trees), cycads, gnetophytes, and *Ginkgo*, none of which have flowers or fruits. Gymnosperms are typically tough and hearty. Their woody pulp, thick bark, branches, and needles or frondlike leaves are difficult to chew. Herbivorous dinosaurs of the Jurassic Period—including the sauropods, stegosaurs, and ankylosaurs—developed jaws, teeth, and digestive systems capable of extracting nutrition from the likes of evergreens, cycads, and other tough gymnosperms. The animals' basic digestive strategy was to minimize chewing of the food in the mouth and to use a fermentation process in the stomach to slowly extract nourishment from the nutritionally stingy gymnosperms.

Gymnosperms were successful at surviving in a Jurassic world with a moderately warm and arid climate. They relied only on wind to carry pollen to their seeds. Pollinated gymnosperm seeds grew slowly, and when fully grown they often took the form of tall trees in species such as ginkgos and conifers. Slow growth and height discouraged consumption by **herbivores**. Sauropod dinosaurs adapted by growing taller to reach the ever-more-lofty canopies of gymnosperms and also developed consumption habits that allowed them to eat fairly constantly in order to derive enough sustenance from the nutritionally stingy conifers and cycads.

(continues on page 28)

THINK ABOUT IT

Dinosaurs of the Poles

The polar regions of today's world are the coldest and harshest on the planet. Most kinds of organisms would not survive for long if left to fend for themselves above the Arctic Circle or in Antarctica. The polar regions of the Earth were not always so uninhabitable, however, and there is growing evidence that a wide variety of dinosaurs lived within the polar circles of the Mesozoic.

Even though the middle latitudes of the Earth were uniformly warm during the Mesozoic Era, temperatures at the poles would have been somewhat cooler, even without the presence of ice caps. Studies of fossil plants and associated oxygen isotope studies of polar sediments have been carried out to determine the average annual temperatures of the Mesozoic polar regions. Results suggest that the North Pole had a mean average temperature between 36° and 46°F (2° and 8 °C) and the South Pole about 50 °F (10 °C)—not tropical temperatures by any means, but not below freezing, either. Another factor affecting life on the extreme ends of the planet would have been prolonged periods of darkness and cooler temperatures still during winter.

The idea that dinosaurs could have lived at the relatively cool poles of the Earth was virtually unthinkable 50 years ago because of the widespread belief that their metabolism was more like that of cold-blooded modern reptiles than that of birds or mammals. The work of **paleontologists** to collect fossils in these regions during the past 20 years has led to a change of thinking. Not only did dinosaurs colonize the poles by at least 190 million years ago, but fragmentary remains have now been identified there for nearly all major branches of the dinosaur evolutionary tree, with the notable and interesting exception of sauropods.

"Polar" dinosaurs—as defined by paleontologists Thomas Rich (Museum of Victoria, Australia); Roland Gangloff (University of Alaska); and William Hammer (Augustana College, Illinois)—are defined as those dinosaurs "that lived within the polar circles of their time, not necessarily within the current polar circles." This means that their fossils are sometimes found on landmasses that have since drifted to the fringes of the ancient polar circles, such as Australia and New Zealand in the south and Alaska, Russia, and the Canadian Yukon in the north.

One of the most productive fossil sites for polar dinosaurs is found on the banks of the Colville River in northeast Alaska. Evidence of polar dinosaurs is usually scant. The most complete dinosaur from any polar locality was found at the Matanuska Formation of south-central Alaska in 1995 and consisted of about a quarter of the animal. Bones from the foot, limbs, and tail were enough to convince paleontologist Anne Pasch of the University of Alaska that what had been found was a specimen of a hadrosaur—a duck-billed dinosaur. Dating of the fossil sediments was made easier by the presence of sea creatures such as ammonites, the age of which can be fixed at about 90 million years ago. That's about 10 million years older than other hadrosaurs from North America and suggests that the Alaskan duckbill might be linked to early hadrosaurs from Asia. Finding the bones of terrestrial animals in marine deposits is not so unusual, although the specimens are usually spotty and incomplete. Pasch speculated that the hadrosaur died on the shore of an ancient ocean and "floated out to sea, probably as a bloated carcass. It eventually sank to the bottom and was buried in fine black mud along with shells and other sea creatures" found with its bones.

Most main groups of dinosaurs are represented by fossil evidence from regions that would have been polar during the Mesozoic. In the Northern Hemisphere, compelling evidence of hadrosaurs, horned dinosaurs, large and small theropods, sauropods, and plated and armored dinosaurs is found in the northern reaches of Alaska, Canada, and Siberia. In the Southern Hemisphere, polar dinosaurs are represented by specimens of armored dinosaurs, small ornithopods, hadrosaurs, prosauropods, sauropods, large and small theropods, and possible horned dinosaurs. These remains are not alone and are often found with fossils of other creatures

(continues)

(continued)

from the polar neighborhood such as crocodilians, amphibians, pterosaurs, birds, and small mammals.

The presence of polar dinosaurs cannot be denied but raises questions about their lifestyle, metabolism, and thermoregulation. Chief among these questions is whether the presence of dinosaurs in cooler regions of the world is evidence of a more active, energetic thermoregulatory metabolism, or whether there was more to the story. Australian paleontologists Thomas Rich and Patricia Vickers Rich, who have done much to advance knowledge of polar dinosaurs of the Southern Hemisphere, speculate that some small dinosaurs may have actually burrowed into the ground to protect themselves against the chill of the long winter nights. Another plausible idea is that some dinosaur groups migrated to the south toward the poles during seasonally warmer periods and returned toward the Equator when the winter chill set in. That would have been possible given the configuration of connected landmasses during much of the Mesozoic. Another clue to dinosaur survival in colder climates might also be related to the possible use of feathers as a form of body insulation—at least for small theropods for which such body coverings have been found.

(continued from page 25)

The dominance of gymnosperms diminished during the Cretaceous Period with the rise of flowering plants—the **angiosperms**. Angiosperms were characterized by a new reproductive life cycle that quickened their ability to grow, breed, and disperse. Angiosperms utilize flowers to attract pollinating animals, such as insects, and also encase their seeds in fruits that, when separated from the plant, can aid in dispersal of seeds. The innovations of flowers to aid in pollination and fruits to protect the embryo contributed to the rapid success and spread of flowering plants. The oldest known

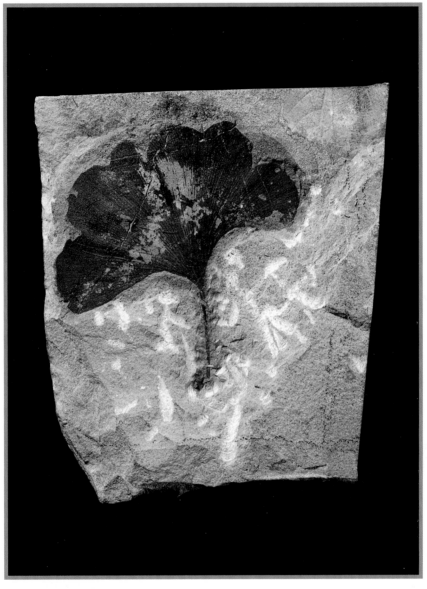

A fossil of a gymnosperm

angiosperm dates from the Early Cretaceous Period, about 125 million years ago. Found in the same Chinese fossil region that contains exciting fossils of early marsupial and placental mammals, feathered dinosaurs, and birds, this primitive early example of a flowering

A fossil of an angiosperm

plant had paired stamens (the pollen-producing parts of a plant) and multiseeded fruits, although it may have lacked flowers.

Angiosperms quickly became a favorite food of dinosaurs. Flowering plants reproduced much more quickly than gymnosperms; angiosperms constantly replenished a landscape that could become heavily browsed by hungry dinosaurs. The ability of angiosperms to grow rapidly and disperse widely allowed them to diversify into hundreds of species by the end of the Cretaceous Period. The

An early magnolia from the Cretaceous Period

importance of the angiosperms to the evolution of dinosaurs cannot be understated. The Cretaceous Period is known for an explosion of new lines of ornithischians—duck-billed, armored, and horned dinosaurs in particular—that developed specialized adaptations for chewing and consuming the wider assortment of vegetation available to them, including the recently evolved flowering plants and gymnosperms. Those special anatomical features will be explored in Section Three of *Last of the Dinosaurs*, in the discussion of ornithischians of the Cretaceous Period.

SUMMARY

This chapter described widespread changes to ocean and land environments, including changes to climates and the rise of flowering plants, that served as catalysts for the spread of dinosaurs and other vertebrates.

1. Continental drift during the Cretaceous Period caused the continued breakup of the northern and southern supercontinents of Laurasia and Gondwana respectively, separating the continents into landmasses approximating their present-day configuration.

2. There was a dramatic rise in sea level during the Cretaceous Period, caused by an acceleration of seafloor spreading that enlarged ocean ridges, formed undersea mountains, and displaced water to areas that were once dry land. Some continental landmasses, including North America, were encroached on by large bodies of water.

3. There were probably no ice caps during the Cretaceous Period, and fossil evidence of plants and animals across the continents from pole to pole strongly suggests that subtropical climates had reached well into the interior of continents of both the Northern and Southern Hemispheres.

4. The dominance of gymnosperms diminished during the Cretaceous Period with the rise of flowering plants—the angiosperms. The ability of angiosperms to grow rapidly and disperse widely allowed them to diversify into hundreds of species by the end of the Cretaceous Period.

5. The rise of angiosperms was accompanied by the corresponding evolution of increasingly efficient and complex dental batteries—adaptations for chewing—in the ornithopod dinosaurs.

SECTION TWO:
SAURISCHIAN
DINOSAURS OF THE
CRETACEOUS PERIOD

2

THE SAUROPODS DIVERSIFY

Sauropods were the largest of all dinosaurs, pushing the anatomical, physiological, and metabolic extremes of terrestrial vertebrates to the upper limits. Sauropods included the tallest, heaviest, and longest land animals to ever walk the Earth.

Sauropods were members of the clade known as **Sauropodomorpha** ("lizard foot form"). This clade is part of a larger clade—the **Saurischia**. Evolutionary adaptations in body size have never been pushed to the anatomical, physiological, and metabolic extremes that were present in the largest of the sauropodomorphs.

The clade Sauropodomorpha included two groups that had a common ancestor but then diverged on two separate lines of large, herbivorous dinosaurs. The earliest group was the Prosauropoda, which lived during the Late Triassic and Early Jurassic Epochs before being supplanted by the second group, the Sauropoda. The "prosauropods" are decribed in detail in *Dawn of the Dinosaur Age*, a companion volume in this series, *The Prehistoric Earth*. The sauropods have roots in the Late Triassic but did not begin to radiate widely until the Early Jurassic. Their most explosive period of evolution occurred during the Middle and Late Jurassic Epochs and is recounted in another volume in this series, *Time of the Giants*. Several lines of sauropods continued to thrive worldwide during the Cretaceous Period, and they are the subjects of this chapter.

SAUROPODS OF THE CRETACEOUS PERIOD

All sauropods had a generally similar body plan featuring a small head, a long neck, a huge body, quadrupedal posture, and a long tail.

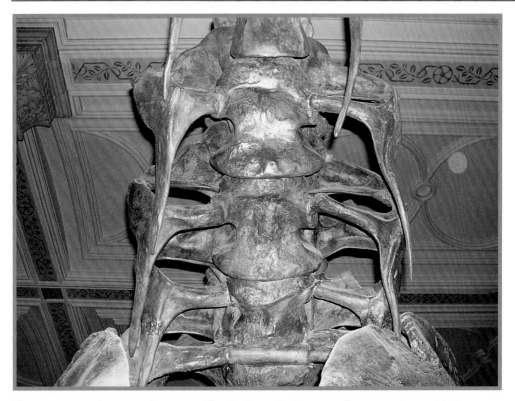

The presence of pneumatic concavities in the spinal bones of sauropods provided lightness without sacrificing strength.

Traits that united the sauropods included sturdy, upright limbs to support their massive weight; four or more fused or **sacral vertebrae** connecting the spine to the pelvic bones; strong, weight-bearing feet; elongation of the neck; a U-shaped mouth opening optimized for stripping vegetation from stems and tree branches; and pneumatic concavities in their spinal bones that provided lightness without sacrificing strength and may also have housed air sacs that were involved in these animals' breathing. Though possessing these similarities, sauropods also developed significant variation that resulted in the evolution of several distinct groups. These groups were mostly distinguished by anatomical differences of the skulls, vertebrae, and limbs.

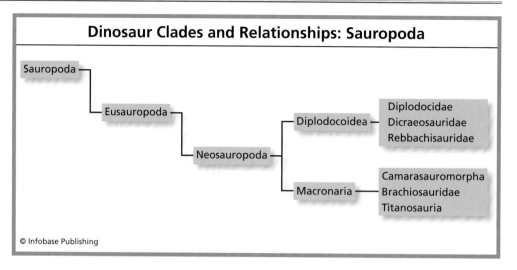

Dinosaur Clades and Relationships: Sauropoda

© Infobase Publishing

Sauropods are divided into several subgroups, as shown in the accompanying figure depicting the evolutionary relationships of the Sauropodomorpha.

Of these sauropod groups, only the Neosauropoda definitely had subgroups that survived into the Cretaceous Period. The **basal** Sauropoda—including the most primitive sauropods, such as *Blikanasaurus* (Late Triassic, South Africa) and *Vulcanodon* (Early Jurassic, Zimbabwe)—lived during the Late Triassic and Early Jurassic. The basal Eusauropoda, whose members still retained some primitive characteristics, lived from the Early Jurassic to the Late Jurassic and are known from more than nine genera, including *Shunosaurus* (Middle Jurassic, China); *Barapasaurus* (Middle Jurassic, India); *Patagosaurus* (Middle Jurassic, Argentina); *Turiasaurus* (Late Jurassic, Spain); and the very-long-necked *Omeisaurus* (Middle Jurassic, China) and *Mamenchisaurus* (Late Jurassic, China).

Neosauropoda is the third major group of sauropods; the clade was made up of the largest number of **taxa** as well as the best known. Many neosauropods date from before the Cretaceous Period, including such iconic dinosaurs as the long and slender diplodocids (*Apatosaurus* and *Diplodocus,* Late Jurassic, western North America); the tall and bulky brachiosaurs (*Brachiosaurus*, Late Jurassic, Tanzania, western United States); and the stocky camarasaurs (*Camarasaurus,* western North America).

Although a few members of the Brachiosauridae and odd relatives of diplodocids have been found in rocks dating from the Early and mid-Cretaceous, the success story of Cretaceous sauropods truly belongs to the Titanosauria, a line of robust, wide-bodied, long-necked plant eaters that became widely distributed, especially in Europe, the Southern Hemisphere, and Asia, and whose last members are found in deposits dating from the Late Cretaceous, at the very end of the time of the dinosaurs. The geographic distribution of these sauropods and their best-known members are described below.

Evolution and Geography: The Geographic Distribution of the Sauropods

The discovery of fossils gives us the only hard facts about the distribution of dinosaurs across the Mesozoic Earth. As such, an understanding of dinosaur distribution is strongly dependent on the availability of fossils, which is subject, in turn, to the availability of fossil deposits of Mesozoic age. The time of the dinosaurs spanned an enormous gulf in time—164 million years—composing the better part of three long geologic periods: the Triassic, the Jurassic, and the Cretaceous.

There is a natural and unavoidable bias in the fossil record that affects the availability of fossils. Paleontologists speak of bias in the fossil record to explain why some forms of prehistoric life are more likely to become fossilized than others. The likelihood that an organism will become a fossil depends on a combination of factors, including the living conditions and anatomical form of the organism as well as the way in which it died. When compared with other organisms, vertebrates have a preservational advantage because their **anatomy** includes an abundance of hard, bony parts. The large size of many dinosaur bones also makes their discovery more likely. The best of skeletons may never be discovered, however, if they are not deposited in a location that is easily accessible to paleontologists.

The surface of the Earth was subject to great geologic change during the Mesozoic and the following Cenozoic. As a consequence, not all of the terrestrial environments that were once occupied by dinosaurs have been preserved at the surface of today's world. Pick any continent, and you will find numerous gaps in the stratigraphic record of dinosaurs. In eastern North America, there are no dinosaur-bearing deposits available that span a 55 million-year-gap from the Early Jurassic to the Early Cretaceous epochs. In South America, evidence of dinosaurs from the Early Jurassic and Late Jurassic Epochs is virtually unknown. Evidence of dinosaurs in China for the entire Late Triassic and Jurassic Epochs is mostly nonexistent. Dinosaurs of Australia are known only from the Middle Jurassic and Early Cretaceous Epochs, while the few Antarctic dinosaurs that have been found date only to the Early Jurassic and Late Cretaceous. Late Cretaceous dinosaurs from Africa are very poorly known, while Indian and Malagasy dinosaurs are almost totally unknown from the Late Jurassic to the mid-Cretaceous. Even in western North America, probably the best-sampled region for dinosaurs in the world, dinosaurs from the Middle Jurassic are essentially unknown.

Add to these geologic gaps in the record of dinosaurs the factor of nonrecovery of fossils that might actually be there, and it would appear that the full extent of dinosaur diversity and **populations** can never be known for certain. Paleontologists currently have validated about 500 dinosaur genera, almost half of which have been described since 1990. Considering that this number represents only the kinds of dinosaurs that have been accessible to science because of various natural biases affecting preservation, the number of actual dinosaur genera that may have existed, including those that have yet to be discovered, is estimated to be between 1,500 and 2,000.

The known geographic distribution of sauropods is naturally affected by the biases just described. Western North America is famous for its wealth of sauropod specimens from the Late Jurassic, but because the fossil record of Early Cretaceous dinosaurs is so poor on much of the continent, little is known of North American sauropods that transitioned into the Early Cretaceous. This is not to say that sauropods disappeared from North America during the Early Cretaceous, but that paleontologists merely have less evidence for them because of the scarcity of fossil deposits of the appropriate age.

Even given a bias in the fossil record toward the discovery of sauropods outside of North America, the Cretaceous Period represents a definite shift in the anatomical adaptations and evolutionary success of some sauropod groups over others. Gone were the diplodocids, camarasaurs, and most of the brachiosaurs—the bulky giants that towered over all other life-forms. In their place was a proliferation of stockier and often smaller sauropods, including the titanosaurs. The transition from the Jurassic to the Cretaceous seems to have been a defining time for the future of sauropods. Their numbers gradually diminished in the Northern Hemisphere until, by the Late Cretaceous, more than 80 percent of known sauropods hailed from regions in the Southern Hemisphere that included South America, Africa, Madagascar, and India (then in a transitional stage, moving from the Southern to the Northern Hemisphere). One thing can be said for certain: The number and diversity of sauropods gradually diminished during the Cretaceous Period, even as the success of the herbivorous ornithopods and ceratopsians and feathered dinosaurs, large theropods, and birds raged.

The reason for this change in the fortune of Northern Hemisphere sauropods is not fully understood. American paleontologist Spencer Lucas suggests that the fate of sauropods might be tied to two related developments in the world of dinosaurs: The rise of flowering plants and the evolution and diversification of ornithopod dinosaurs adapted to eat such flowering plants. The fact that sauropods changed little in their eating adaptations might mean that they were poorly adapted to eat and digest flowering plants even as the range of tall gymnosperm trees began to slacken, outcompeted by angiosperms. Sauropods also may have had difficulty competing for what plant material was left for them because of the growing numbers of ornithopods that could eat practically anything, tough-skinned evergreens and flowering plants alike. Lucas notes that the relative scarcity of ornithopod fossils in the Southern Hemisphere corresponds with a stronger presence of sauropods in continents below the Equator during the Late Cretaceous Epoch. A lack of success of ornithopods in the southern continents might help explain the abundance of the sauropods in those locations.

Cretaceous Sauropods

The sauropod group Neosauropoda is subdivided into two major clades: the Diplodocoidea (comprising the Rebbachisauridae, Dicraeosauridae, and Diplodocidae) and the Macronaria (composed mainly of the Camarasauridae, Brachiosauridae, and Titanosauria). Of these, only the Macronaria had taxa that survived into the Early and Late Cretaceous Epochs as members of the brachiosaurs and titanosaurs. The Macronaria were distinguished from other sauropods by skull features that included a nasal opening that was larger than the eye opening. In contrast to the Diplodocoidea, macronarians were generally larger, taller, and bulkier sauropods. They were also typically stockier and heavier than the slender, whip-tailed diplodocids and their kin.

Brachiosaurs

Brachiosaurs were distinguished by extremely long necks and by forelimbs that were longer than their **hind limbs**—a body plan different from that of other kinds of sauropods. This anatomy gave brachiosaurs great height, and some members of this clade are considered the tallest of all dinosaurs. Only a few brachiosaur genera are currently recognized. The most famous is *Brachiosaurus* itself, which dates from the Late Jurassic of Tanzania and the western United States and is known from some magnificent specimens, including a composite skeleton mounted in the Museum für Naturkunde in Berlin, Germany. It is the largest real mounted dinosaur skeleton in the world. Two other recently described genera of brachiosaurs lived in the Early Cretaceous Epoch and were discovered in the United States.

Cedarosaurus (Early Cretaceous, Utah) is known from a partial **postcranial** skeleton—a specimen lacking the head. Described in

1999, the original specimen of *Cedarosaurus* is also notable for having been associated with a small cluster of 115 so-called **gastroliths**, or "stomach stones." The rounded stones were discovered within the body cavity of *Cedarosaurus* and were originally interpreted as being part of a gastric mill in a birdlike gizzard of the sauropod, an interpretation that has since been refuted. Current research comparing sauropods to other tetrapods concludes that the largest of the dinosaurs probably relied on a simple bacterial fermentation process and a slow digestive process to extract nutrients from their food. The stones found with the specimen of *Cedarosaurus* may have simply been swallowed accidentally by the dinosaur.

Sauroposeidon lived during the Early Cretaceous Epoch and was found in Oklahoma. First described in 2000, the specimen consists only of four neck vertebrae, but these are so closely similar to those of other brachiosaurs that the *Sauroposeidon*'s classification as a member of this clade can be claimed with near certainty. A key difference in the neck vertebrae of *Sauroposeidon* is that they are elongated by about 25 percent more than comparable vertebrae in *Brachiosaurus*; this indicates that the last of the known brachiosaurs had continued the trend towards longer and longer necks. Assuming that *Sauroposeidon* was much like *Brachiosaurus* in all other respects, a hypothetical reconstruction on paper would make *Sauroposeidon* about 60 feet (18 m) tall, which is about 25 percent taller than the most complete specimen of *Brachiosaurus* in the Museum für Naturkunde in Berlin. The long neck of *Sauroposeidon* is also a record holder among dinosaurs. Measuring about 40 feet (12 m) long, *Sauroposeidon*'s neck was longer than those of all other known sauropods. There are a few sauropods that may have had a neck nearly as long—for example, large specimens of *Mamenchisaurus* and the newly named Patagonian titanosaurs *Futalognkosaurus* and *Puertasaurus*.

Not all paleontologists agree that brachiosaurs raised their heads to such heights. For those who believe in this, however, the presumed upstretched posture and extreme height of brachiosaurs raises some interesting questions about the physiological challenges of pumping

The neck of *Sauroposeidon* was the longest of all known sauropods.

blood to the elevated head. This posture is unlike most quadrupedal terrestrial vertebrates, whose heads are normally carried at about the same level as the heart—the giraffe being an informative exception. In the giraffe, the heart is much larger than that in mammals of similar mass, enabling the animal to pump blood upwards to its elevated head. Special valves in the neck open and close to prevent blood from rushing up and down the neck as the giraffe raises and lowers its head.

By comparison, if a brachiosaur had a similar circulatory system, its heart would have been massive in order to maintain the pressure needed to pump blood to the brain. British paleontologist David Norman (b. 1941) further explained that the brachiosaur heart was probably divided into two parts: one for generating the high pressure needed to pump blood to the head, and the other, requiring much lower pressure, to pump blood into the lungs. A two-part heart such as this is also found in mammals (including the giraffe) and birds, but is only imperfectly present in extant reptiles; this further suggests that dinosaurs had closer affinities with the **physiology** of mammals and birds than with cold-blooded reptiles.

Basal Titanosaurs

The last surviving group of sauropods were titanosaurs, and their distribution was nearly worldwide. Titanosaurs had roots in the Late Jurassic of Tanzania, Thailand, and western North America. Although specimens have been found all over the world, most titanosaur remains are fragmentary and lack skull elements. The most complete specimens have been found in Argentina and Madagascar, where the recent discoveries of two exquisite skulls have enabled paleontologists to better understand the evolution of these sauropods.

Anatomical traits found in all titanosaurs included a **sacrum** consisting of at least six fused vertebrae; hind limbs that were spread more widely than those of other sauropods; relatively small feet; and enlarged breastbones. Their front limbs were reduced in length compared to those of other sauropods. Unique among sauropods, many titanosaurs had ball-and-socket joints between their tailbones; that is, a "ball" of bone on one vertebra fit into a "socket" on the next. The tail was usually short and the neck of medium length.

The skulls of titanosaurs have rarely been found, although a few fine examples have recently been unearthed. In Argentina, paleontologist Rubén Martínez recovered an isolated titanosaur skull and neck from the earliest Late Cretaceous badlands of Chubut Province in central Patagonia. Around the same time, in 2001, American paleontologists Kristina Curry Rogers and Catherine A. Forster described a remarkably complete skeleton and skulls of a medium-sized titanosaur from the Late Cretaceous of Madagascar that they named *Rapetosaurus* ("mischievous giant lizard"), after a figure from Malagasy folklore. The best-known specimen of *Rapetosaurus* is a juvenile that measured about 30 feet (9 m) long. The skull of *Rapetosaurus* and the skull of the as yet-unnamed Argentinean specimen found by Martínez are most similar to those skulls

Rapetosaurus is known for the most complete skeleton of a titanosaur found to date.

of the diplodocids, with nostrils positioned high on the skull and a U-shaped jaw equipped with peglike teeth for plucking vegetation positioned in the front of the mouth. In contrast, the as yet-unnamed Argentinean titanosaur found by Martínez most closely resembles that of *Brachiosaurus* and in many ways seems to be an intermediate between brachiosaurids and later titanosaurs.

Titanosaurs are also known for representing the opposite ends of the size scale for sauropods. *Magyarosaurus* (Late Cretaceous, Romania) is among the smallest known adult specimens of a sauropod. It was a dwarf species whose maximum length was about 20 feet (6.2 m). In contrast, the largest of all known dinosaurs was also a titanosaur. *Argentinosaurus* (Late Cretaceous, Argentina) is known from only a partial skeleton, but it appears to have been the most massive of dinosaurs, weighing about 82 tons (70 metric tons) and measuring about 120 feet (36 m) long.

Other well-known members of the titanosaurs have been found in widely distant geographic locations and include:

North America
Alamosaurus (Late Cretaceous, New Mexico, Utah, Texas)

Europe
Lirainosaurus (Late Cretaceous, Spain)
Ampelosaurus (Late Cretaceous, France)

Asia
Huabeisaurus (Late Cretaceous, China)
Nemegtosaurus (Late Cretaceous, Mongolia)
Opisthocoelicaudia (Late Cretaceous, Mongolia)
Quaesitosaurus (Late Cretaceous, Mongolia)
Phuwiangosaurus (Early Cretaceous, Thailand)

Central Asia
Isisaurus (Late Cretaceous, India)
Jainosaurus (Late Cretaceous, India)

South America
Chubutisaurus (Early Cretaceous, Argentina)
Ligabuesaurus (Early Cretaceous, Argentina)
Aeolosaurus (Late Cretaceous, Argentina)
Andesaurus (Late Cretaceous, Argentina)

(continues on page 48)

THINK ABOUT IT

The Largest Dinosaur

The title of largest—or, more appropriately, most massive—dinosaur is currently held by *Argentinosaurus*, an enormous titanosaur from the Late Cretaceous of Argentina that is known from only a very incomplete skeleton. Conservative estimates place its weight at about 82 tons (70 metric tons) and its length at about 120 feet (36 m) or more. It was neither the tallest nor the longest dinosaur—records that are currently held by *Sauroposeidon* and *Supersaurus*, respectively—but it was the heaviest and most massive based on reasonably good fossil evidence.

Dinosaur paleontology has its share of legends and myths, and none is more intriguing than the mystery of the "one that got away": the remains of a gigantic sauropod discovered in the nineteenth century, that, if ever confirmed, would dwarf even *Argentinosaurus*.

In 1878, the fossil-hunting team of American paleontologist Edward Drinker Cope (1840–1897) was unearthing plentiful remains of sauropod dinosaurs in Colorado. Many of the specimens represented were quite complete, providing the first good look at the anatomy of sauropods. In one case, however, Cope's crew uncovered only a single vertebra from an enormous backbone. Nothing else of this animal was found, but the vertebra resembled that of smaller, known sauropods. Cope remarked that it was the "largest saurian" he had yet seen, and he published a brief account of the find along with a drawing of the bone. He believed that the vertebra was from a larger specimen of a sauropod he had previously described, *Amphicoelias*, whose name means "biconcave," in reference to the concave shape of its vertebrae.

The vertebra was incomplete but clearly that of the back area of a true giant among giants. Cope's sketch, in which he outlined the missing elements of the vertebra, showed that it would have measured about 7.9 feet (2.7 m) tall when complete. By comparison, a similar vertebra from the 30-ton sauropod *Apatosaurus* is only about half as tall at 4 feet (1.2 m). Even in those early days of dinosaur science, Cope knew that he had found a remarkable creature. He wrote that in "the extreme tenuity of all its parts, this vertebra exceeds those of this type already

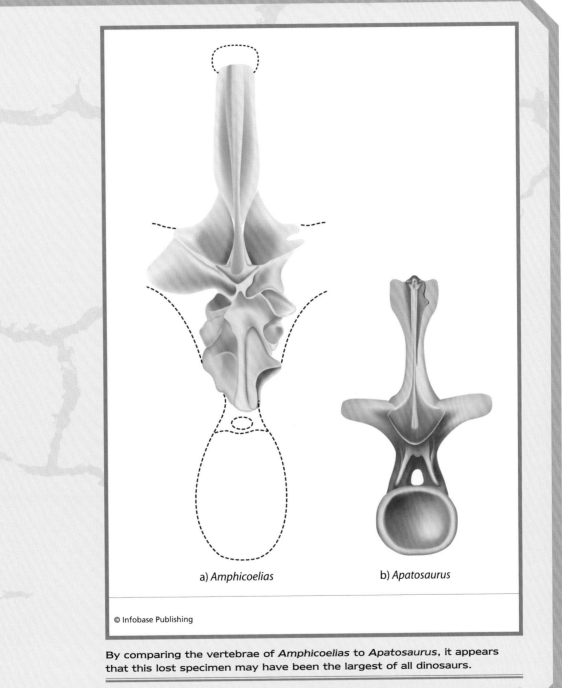

a) *Amphicoelias*   b) *Apatosaurus*

By comparing the vertebrae of *Amphicoelias* to *Apatosaurus*, it appears that this lost specimen may have been the largest of all dinosaurs.

(continues)

(continued)

described. . . . The dimensions of its vertebra much exceed those of any known land animal."

Using as a basis for comparison the kinds of diplodocid sauropods that this vertebra most closely resembled, estimates for the size and bulk of *Amphicoelias* suggest that it could have weighed up to 135 tons (122 metric tons) and could have been up to 191 feet long (58 m). This would make *Amphicoelias* more than 50 tons (45 metric tons) heavier than *Argentinosaurus* and at least 50 feet (15 m) longer than *Supersaurus*. Unfortunately, the vertebra of *Amphicoelias* apparently crumbled to pieces while in transport and storage and no longer exists, making the case for this record holder impossible to verify.

(continued from page 45)

Antarctosaurus (Late Cretaceous, Argentina)
Bonitasaura (Late Cretaceous, Argentina)
Epachthosaurus (Late Cretaceous, Argentina)
Futalognkosaurus (Late Cretaceous, Argentina)
Mendozasaurus (Late Cretaceous, Argentina)
Muyelensaurus (Late Cretaceous, Argentina)
Puertasaurus (Late Cretaceous, Argentina)
Rinconsaurus (Late Cretaceous, Argentina)
Baurutitan (Late Cretaceous, Brazil)
Trigonosaurus (Late Cretaceous, Brazil)

Africa
Malawisaurus (Early Cretaceous, Malawi)
Janenschia (Late Jurassic, Tanzania)
Paralititan (Late Cretaceous, Egypt)
Aegyptosaurus (Late Cretaceous, Egypt)

The renaissance in knowledge of titanosaurs experienced another spike in 1998, when a joint team of American and Argentinean paleontologists discovered a rich deposit of titanosaur eggs and nests in northwestern Argentina. As many as 195 egg clusters were found, as well as the complete skeletons of embryonic titanosaurs, some isolated remains of adult titanosaurs, and specimens of theropods that probably preyed on the sauropods and their young. Each cluster of eggs contained a half-dozen or more eggs. Each egg was only about 5 or 6 inches in diameter and nearly round. The egg nests were layered in such a way that it became clear that titanosaurs returned to the site on a seasonal basis to lay their eggs.

Saltasaurs

Including four genera found to date, the Saltasaurinae are considered to be the most **derived** titanosaurs. Saltasaurs have been thought of as the armored sauropods because of evidence that their backs and sides were sparsely studded with a matrix of protective, bony knobs. This protection was not extensive enough to have offered much protection, so the function of such bony nodules may have merely been for visual display.

Other distinguishing features of saltasaurs are found in the morphology of the animals' vertebrae and forelimbs. Saltasaurs had short tails, small feet, six or sometimes seven sacral vertebrae, and a wide, deep division along the tops of the vertebrae between the **neural spines**. Saltasaurs were moderately long, measuring between 20 and 35 feet (6 and 11 m). Saltasaurines are known with certainty only from the Late Cretaceous of Argentina and include *Saltasaurus*, *Neuquensaurus*, *Rocasaurus*, and *Bonatitan* (Late Cretaceous, Argentina); and *Opisthocoelicaudia* (Late Cretaceous, Mongolia).

LAST OF THE SAUROPODS

Like all of the non-avian dinosaurs, sauropods perished at the end of the Late Cretaceous Epoch. Reasons for the mass extinction of dinosaurs and many other **fauna** at that time are explored in the conclusion of *Last of the Dinosaurs*. As for the sauropods, their long history, with roots in the Late Triassic Epoch, is one of tremendous success and adaptive persistence. Aside from body size, skull and tooth shape, and the relative length of the forelimbs and neck, sauropods shared many similarities throughout their history. Among these were jaws and teeth capable of plucking but not chewing vegetation and an apparent digestive process that utilized a long and slow fermentation process in the gut. Sauropods developed these eating adaptations during the Triassic or Jurassic Period, when their world was dominated by gymnosperms such as evergreen trees. Sauropods adapted a variety of successful eating adaptations during their long history and persisted in a variety of diverse, although diminishing, forms, until the end of the Cretaceous Period when the last of the dinosaurs became extinct.

Of the roughly 100 or more valid sauropod genera spanning the entire Age of Dinosaurs, as many as 35 date from the end of the Late Cretaceous alone. The last stand of the sauropods was exclusively that of the diverse and geographically widespread titanosaurs, perhaps the biggest success story of all the sauropod clans. While the greatest number of titanosaur specimens are associated with the Southern Hemisphere, many Late Cretaceous titanosaurs have been found in the Northern Hemisphere, including Utah, New Mexico, and Texas (*Alamosaurus*); Spain (*Lirainosaurus*); France (*Ampelosaurus*); Romania (*Magyarosaurus*), China (*Huabeisaurus, Sonidosaurus*); and Mongolia (*Quaesitosaurus, Nemegtosaurus, Opisthocoelicaudia*).

One of the genuine puzzles regarding sauropods was their large body size, a trait that persisted from their origins to their **extinction**. While the gigantism of sauropods may be seen as the ultimate extension of a tendency toward large body size in many kinds of dinosaurs, one can also ponder why these extremes never dominated the evolution of mammals to the same extent. Sauropods developed large body size to a degree never seen before or since in terrestrial vertebrate faunas. Many hypotheses exist for why this was, taking into account such diverse factors as thermoregulation, climate, competitive advantage in the herbivory, and defense. In 1995, a team of paleontologists that included James Farlow, Peter Dodson, and Anusuya Chinsamy-Turan took a comprehensive look at all of these factors leading to gigantism in dinosaurs. While acknowledging that gigantism is linked to a complex of interrelated physiological and ecological circumstances, the team concluded that the key factor affecting dinosaur gigantism was that they required less food than hypothetical mammals of equally gigantic proportions. Less-demanding food requirements would have improved the chances for such giant dinosaurs to maintain large populations, to survive whatever disasters fell upon them, and to further their species.

This amalgam of ideas speaks to the mystery that is at the core of dinosaur science. It is difficult to understand fully how such gigantic animals could have existed based only on our understanding of living species in today's world. Dinosaurs were biologically unique, and a failure to fully understand the mechanisms behind their growth, thermoregulation, size, and lifestyle is due only to the limitations of present-day science and the incompleteness of the fossil record. One thing is certain: A failure to understand dinosaurs should not be interpreted as meaning that dinosaurs were a failure. Dinosaurs existed for more than 160 million years as one of life's greatest success stories.

SUMMARY

This chapter discussed the several lines of sauropods that continued to thrive worldwide during the Cretaceous Period.

1. Sauropods of the Cretaceous Period include members of the clades Brachiosauridae, Titanosauria, Rebbachisauridae, and Dicraeosauridae.
2. The Cretaceous Period represents a shift in the anatomical adaptations and evolutionary success of some sauropod families over others. Their numbers gradually diminished in the Northern Hemisphere until, by the Late Cretaceous, more than 80 percent of known sauropods hailed from regions in the Southern Hemisphere.

3. Sauropods may have diminished in areas where they had to compete with other numerous herbivores such as horned dinosaurs and duck-billed dinosaurs. Sauropods also may have been less adapted to eating flowering plants, which began to dominate the Cretaceous floras.

4. The last surviving group of sauropods were titanosaurs, and their distribution was nearly worldwide.

5. Of the 100 or so valid sauropod genera spanning the entire Age of Dinosaurs, some 35 date from the end of the Late Cretaceous.

6. One possible explanation for gigantism in sauropods is that their biology had less-demanding food requirements than that of mammals of comparable size, which improved the chances for such dinosaurs to maintain viable populations, to survive whatever disasters fell upon them, and to further the species.

3

Theropod Giants and Feathered Dinosaurs

The story of predatory dinosaurs began during the early stages of dinosaur evolution with the appearance of the first theropods in the Late Triassic Epoch. By the Middle and Late Jurassic Epochs, the evolutionary lineages of meat-eating dinosaurs had diversified dramatically, leading in one direction to such large carnivores as *Allosaurus* (Late Jurassic, western North America) and in another direction to such small, chicken-sized insectivores as *Compsognathus* (Late Jurassic, Germany). The Late Jurassic was also witness to the evolution of the first known bird, *Archaeopteryx* (Late Jurassic, Germany), from theropod ancestors, whose mosaic of traits included wings and feathers as well as a very unbirdlike tail and toothy mouth.

The evolution of theropods was in full bloom during the latter Jurassic, seemingly keeping pace with an ever-broadening array of prey animals, including dinosaurs, insects, lizards, and small mammals. Significant as it was, however, theropod evolution of the Jurassic Period pales in comparison to the truly explosive development of **carnivorous** dinosaurs of many kinds during the Cretaceous Period that followed. The theropods of the Jurassic laid the groundwork for an even greater spurt of predatory dinosaur evolution that led to the development of feathered dinosaurs, hulking meat eaters, swift and agile pursuit predators, ostrichlike dinosaurs, and the largest carnivorous animals ever to walk on land, including *Tyrannosaurus* (Late Cretaceous, western North America); *Giganotosaurus* (Late Cretaceous, Argentina); *Mapusaurus* (Late Cretaceous, Argentina);

Carcharodontosaurus (Late Cretaceous, North Africa); and *Spinosaurus* (Late Cretaceous, North Africa). This chapter explores the last great families of carnivorous dinosaurs that flourished during the Early and Late Cretaceous Epochs.

OVERVIEW OF CRETACEOUS THEROPODS

Carnivorous dinosaurs were members of the saurischian clade known as **Theropoda** ("beast foot"), which included numerous distinct subgroups all sharing a common ancestor. About 40 percent of all known dinosaur taxa were theropods. Their remains have been found on every continent, and theropods ranged in size from the tiniest of dinosaurs to the largest terrestrial predators that ever existed. Another book in this series, *Dawn of the Dinosaur Age,* provides a detailed look at the classification of theropods and the anatomical adaptations that unite all of their taxa.

In evolutionary terms, the theropod group known as the Tetanurae ("stiff tails") represented the last great wave of predatory dinosaurs, as well as birds. The tetanurans were the most birdlike, or derived, of theropods. The name Tetanurae refers to a stiffening of the tail because of interlocking projections on the tail vertebrae. Members of this clade also shared certain modifications, such as a ridge on the shoulder blade for the attachment of muscle, features of the hand, and changes to the leg and knee joint. As a group of related taxa, the tetanurans include modern birds and any theropods that share a more recent common ancestor with birds than with *Ceratosaurus*, which belonged to the earliest and most primitive branches of the evolutionary tree of carnivorous dinosaurs.

For the purposes of discussion, theropods may be defined as all of the descendants of the common ancestor of *Coelophysis* (Late Triassic, New Mexico) and Aves (birds). Accordingly, the following categories are used in this series, *The Prehistoric Earth,* to organize the discussion of theropods:

Ceratosauria (Late Triassic to Late Cretaceous Epochs). These are the most primitive theropods, including theropods more closely related to *Ceratosaurus* than to birds. The Ceratosauria is further divided into two subgroups: Coelophysoidea, consisting

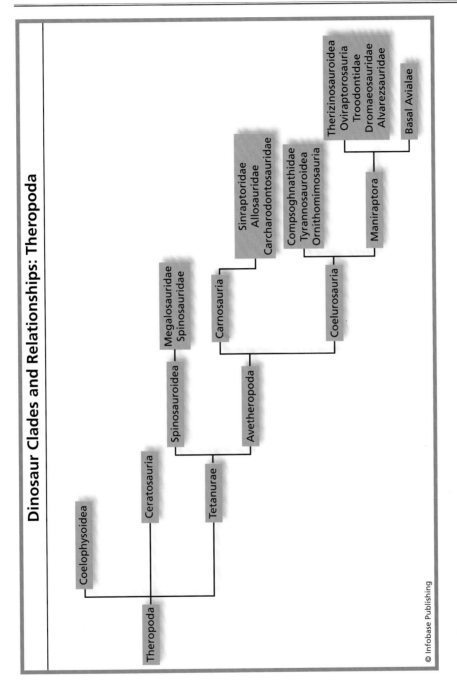

Dinosaur Clades and Relationships: Theropoda

© Infobase Publishing

primarily of small theropods that lived from the Late Triassic to Early Jurassic Epoch, and Neoceratosauria, composed of many medium- to large-bodied theropods, mostly from the Southern

Hemisphere, that lived throughout the Jurassic and Cretaceous and usually exhibited some form of skull ornamentation. Examples of Coelophysoidea and Neoceratosauria from the Late Triassic Epoch and the Jurassic Period are discussed in *Dawn of the Dinosaur Age* and *Time of the Giants,* two other books in this series. The discussion of neoceratosaurs below covers taxa that lived during the Cretaceous Period.

Tetanurae (Middle Jurassic to Late Cretaceous Epochs). These were the most derived, nonceratosaurian theropods. Tetanurans are defined as modern birds and any theropods sharing a more recent common ancestor with birds than with *Ceratosaurus.* The Tetanurae is further divided into two major subgroups: the Spinosauroidea, consisting of the most primitive, least-birdlike, basal tetanurans, and the more derived Avetheropoda. Among the Spinosauroidea were the largest of all theropods, the spinosaurids from North Africa. The Avetheropoda were the most diverse theropod group and included many well-known genera that populated the Northern and Southern Hemispheres during the Cretaceous Period. These included giants such as *Tyrannosaurus, Giganotosaurus, Mapusaurus,* and *Carcharodontosaurus;* ostrich-like dinosaurs; the sickle-clawed dromaeosaurs popularly known as "raptors"; and others, including various taxa of feathered dinosaurs leading to modern birds.

CERATOSAURS OF THE CRETACEOUS

The earliest theropods—the Coelophysoidea—lived during the Late Triassic and Early Jurassic Epochs and represented the first radiation of carnivorous dinosaurs. Several other primitive lines of theropods persisted well into the Late Cretaceous, particularly in regions of the Southern Hemisphere (now Argentina, North Africa, India, and Madagascar). These were the ceratosaurs, many of which exhibited bizarre adaptations not seen in theropods of the Northern Hemisphere.

The body plan of most ceratosaurs included a short, stocky neck, long hind limbs, a stout tail, and strong but short forelimbs tipped with four-fingered hands. The top of the skull of ceratosaurs was often embellished with horns or lumps. Neoceratosaur skulls were also broad at the snout and tall, with a deep **premaxilla** positioned below the nasal openings.

Ceratosaurus (Late Jurassic, Colorado, Wyoming, and Utah), first described in 1884, was one of the first large carnivorous dinosaurs to be well understood. *Ceratosaurus* was a medium to large predator that measured up to 20 feet (6.6 m) long. Recent computed tomography (CT) studies of the braincase of a new specimen of *Ceratosaurus* suggests a posture for the head and neck that was more horizontal than upright, eyesight that was probably about average for a theropod, and a well-formed sense of smell comparable to that of birds.

The Cretaceous ceratosaurian relatives of *Ceratosaurus* are represented by several excellent specimens from the Southern Hemisphere. These ceratosaurian predators were the most abundant theropods of Gondwana during the Late Cretaceous and are known from partial and nearly complete specimens from Argentina, Brazil, North Africa, Madagascar, India, and southern Europe.

Partial remains of large Cretaceous theropods from India were some of the earliest remains of ceratosaurians discovered. Consisting of dissociated bones from the skull, vertebral column, girdles, and limbs, as well as incomplete skeletons, some of these taxa—including *Laevisuchus*, *Indosuchus*, and *Indosaurus*—still remain enigmatic today many years after their discovery in the 1920s and 1930s. A partial skull roof from Madagascar announced in 1979 was originally thought to be that of a dome-headed dinosaur, the likes of which had never been discovered in the Southern Hemisphere. Named *Majungatholus* ("Majunga dome") after a region in Madagascar, its affinities with ceratosaurian predatory dinosaurs would remain a mystery until 1998. This same dinosaur would be re-christened *Majungasaurus*. The discovery in Argentina in the early 1980s of such partial specimens as *Noasaurus* ("northwestern Argentina lizard") and *Xenotarsosaurus* ("strange ankle lizard,"

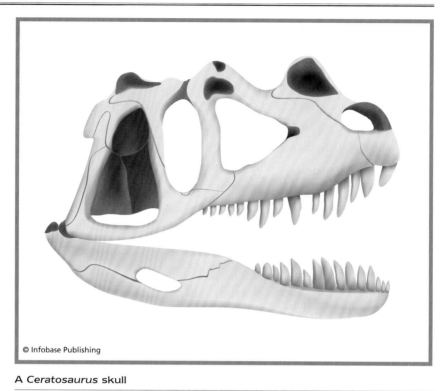

© Infobase Publishing

A *Ceratosaurus* skull

after its unusually fused ankle bones) in the early 1980s encouraged famed Argentine paleontologist José Bonaparte (b. 1928) to expand his fieldwork in the Cretaceous fossil beds of his home country. It was Bonaparte whose breakthrough discoveries of *Carnotaurus* and *Abelisaurus* in the 1980s began to unlatch a window on the history of Gondwanan theropods that had yet to be opened more than a crack.

Carnotaurus (Late Cretaceous, Argentina) is known from a remarkably complete skeleton and skull. It was in some ways an extreme predator, with an exceptionally short and tall skull, a short, strong neck, and a broad muzzle. The name *Carnotaurus* means "meat-eating bull"; the animal was given its name because of the prominent bull-like horns on the brow of each eye. This medium-sized theropod was about 25 feet (7.5 m) long and had a stout, strong neck, forelimbs that were shorter than those of *Tyrannosaurus,* and four claws each instead of the two seen in tyrannosaurs. With its strong legs and muscular jaws and neck, *Carnotaurus* possibly attacked nose first, thrusting its mouth into its prey and ripping flesh away with a turn of its head. On the other hand, the teeth of *Carnotaurus* were remarkably short, and its lower jaws were weak compared to those of most other theropods. Perhaps *Carnotaurus* attacked with its upper jaws in a chopping, axe-like fashion.

While further specimens of *Carnotaurus* have yet to turn up, a similar theropod named *Aucasaurus* (Late Cretaceous, Argentina) was named by Argentine paleontologists Rodolfo Coria and Luis Chiappe and American paleonologist Lowell Dingus in 2002 based on another nearly complete skeleton. *Aucasaurus* was 30 percent smaller than *Carnotaurus,* lacked the brow horn, had a somewhat longer, narrower skull, and also had forelimbs that were somewhat longer than those of its bigger cousin.

The true nature of *Majungasaurus* (previously named *Majungatholus*; Late Cretaceous, Madagascar), once thought to be a bone-headed pachycephalosaur, became evident in the late 1990s when a team of paleontologists led by American David Krause went to Madagascar and uncovered several new partial specimens, including a spectacularly preserved skull. The skull did indeed have a bony knob on top of its head, but it was actually a rounded horn on the forehead, not a skull cap as found in pachycephalosaurs. The skull was tall and blunt nosed, like its ceratosaur cousins from South America. *Majungasaurus* was a medium-sized carnivore measuring about 21 feet (6 m) long with strong hind legs and short, three-clawed forelimbs. A curious discovery among the fossils of *Majungasaurus* were bones with tooth marks that can be attributed to *Majungasaurus* itself; this provided evidence that this theropod may have either fed on its own kind or scavenged dead members of its clan. In either case, this evidence shows that some dinosaurs may have been cannibalistic.

The story of ceratosaurs from Gondwana also includes a theropod with one of the most unusual jaws ever seen in a predatory dinosaur—*Masiakasaurus* (Late Cretaceous, Madagascar). Named in 2001 by a team led by American paleontologist Scott Sampson, *Masiakasaurus* ("vicious lizard") is so named because its teeth protrude outward, especially along the front of the jaws. In some ways, its mouth more closely resembles those of extinct marine reptiles (see Chapter 8), which also suggests that *Masiakasaurus* was adapted to eat fishes, snakes, and other small, scampering animals. Sampson remarked that when they first found the lower jaw, they did not think it was from a dinosaur because they had never seen anything like it. The 6-foot-long (2 m) *Masiakasaurus* turns out to be just one of many bizarre evolutionary sidetracks that took place on the island of Madagascar. That island, along with the India landmass, had separated from the rest of the southern continents during the Cretaceous Period. *Masiakasaurus* is in good company with equally bizarre birdlike dinosaurs (or dinosaurlike birds); blunt-nosed, plant-eating crocodiles; and horned theropods such as *Majungasaurus* that are also found on the island. The complete scientific name of this dinosaur also gives us the rare opportunity to mix dinosaur trivia with rock and roll trivia: The complete name is *Masiakasaurus knopfleri*, in honor of rock guitarist Mark Knopfler, whose music the scientists listened to while digging up the fossils.

TETANURAE OF THE CRETACEOUS PERIOD

Tetanurans make up the largest group and variety of known theropod dinosaurs. The earliest tetanurans arose during the Jurassic Period and do not represent a **monophyletic** group of organisms containing all of the descendants of a single, common ancestor. This is quickly apparent from the wide variation seen in basal tetanurans, which range from one of the smallest known dinosaurs, *Compsognathus*, to the largest known theropods, *Spinosaurus* and *Giganotosaurus*. Some of the traits seen in all basal tetanurans include simple, bladelike teeth (except in spinosaurids, which have conical teeth) and strong, but moderately short, three-fingered forelimbs.

Collectively, this assemblage of creatures is further divided into two larger groups: the Spinosauroidea and the Avetheropoda.

Spinosauroidea

The Spinosauroidea were a group of related theropods considered to be basal within the Tetanurae. The group is further broken down into two smaller groups. The Megalosauridae were medium- to large-sized theropods that mostly lived during the Middle and Late Jurassic Epochs. The Spinosauridae included several large-bodied forms that reigned as the largest carnivores in their ecosystems up until the early part of the Late Cretaceous, at which time they were replaced by more derived tetanurans.

Megalosauridae

The namesake of the Megalosauridae is *Megalosaurus* (Middle Jurassic, England), which has the distinction of being the first dinosaur ever described scientifically. The original specimen of *Megalosaurus* was a partial skeleton that included a lower jaw; it was studied by William Buckland in 1825. The group of dinosaurs that goes by the name of megalosaurids has long been something of a wastebasket for a variety of fragmentary Jurassic theropod remains. While recent work by paleontologists including Thomas Holtz, Ralph Molnar, Philip Currie, and Paul Sereno (b. 1957) has done much to establish a firmer basis for defining theropods of this group, even the best specimens of megalosaurs are only partial and often lack much of the skull and postcranial skeleton. Megalosaurs have been found in England, France, and the United States as well as in Niger and Argentina, thus extending the reach of this clade to the Northern and Southern Hemispheres of the dinosaur world.

One of the most complete megalosaurid specimens is that of *Afrovenator* ("African hunter"), discovered in Niger in 1994. The specimen represents a 30-foot (9 m) predatory dinosaur that lived between 125 million and 136 million years ago. The skull is nearly complete, except for the lower jaw, and the rest of the skeleton reveals a lightly built theropod with strong forelimbs with three robust claws, a trait characteristic of this animal's tetanuran relatives, such as *Allosaurus*. The evolutionary links between *Afrovenator* and megalosaurids from the Northern Hemisphere suggests that a land bridge still existed between the continents above and below the Equator as late as the Early Cretaceous Epoch.

Other noteworthy megalosaurids include *Torvosaurus* (Late Jurassic, Utah, Colorado, and Wyoming); *Piatnitzkysaurus* (Middle Jurassic, Argentina); *Poekilopleuron* (Middle Jurassic, France), *Dubreuillosaurus* (Middle Jurassic, France); and *Eustreptospondylus* (Middle Jurassic, England).

Spinosauridae

For many years, the Spinosauridae were represented only by an enigmatic large predator, *Spinosaurus*, discovered by German paleontologist Baron Ernst Stromer von Reichenbach (1870–1952) of the University of Munich. The story of the discovery of *Spinosaurus* is one of scientific adventure and hardships; it is also the tale of a dinosaur once lost but revealed again nearly six decades later.

The *Spinosaurus* story began when a young Ernst Stromer ventured into a desolate region of the Egyptian desert in 1910. Accompanied only by a guide, a cook, four camels, and two camel drivers, Stromer was hoping to find fossils of early mammals that had previously been discovered in other regions of the Egyptian desert. Instead, he stumbled upon a trove of dinosaur fossils dating from the first part of the Late Cretaceous Epoch, a time when Egypt was green and much wetter.

Stromer hired an experienced fossil hunter named Richard Markgraf to help him recover his finds. In three short years, the two men excavated more than 50 new kinds of animals and plants, including dinosaurs, fishes, turtles, snakes, marine reptiles, and crocodiles. Their rewards did not come easily. Fieldwork was best carried out in the early months of the year, before the onset of the devastating desert heat. Sandstorms were possible in the day or night, and the wind could whip up violently at any time, sending a fine, sandy dust through the air and into the eyes of the workers. Add to all that a veritable plague of camel fleas. It is a wonder that

Stromer and Markgraf lasted as long as they did, working that forbidding landscape for fossils.

The most spectacular of Stromer's dinosaur discoveries was *Spinosaurus* ("spine lizard"), an incredibly large predator that is estimated to have been about 50 to 57 feet (15 to 17 m) long. An unusual feature of *Spinosaurus* were long spines on its back that probably formed a large, sail-like structure. The spines alone were up to 6.6 feet (2 m) tall, adding height to a creature that must have stood about 16 to 20 feet (5 to 6 m) tall at the hips. Of the creature's skull, Stromer found only the lower jaws and a fragment of the upper, but these fossils, too, revealed an unusual trait. Whereas most theropods had bladelike teeth, the teeth of *Spinosaurus* were conical and unserrated, more like those of a crocodile.

Returning to Munich, Stromer mounted his partial skeleton of *Spinosaurus* on a wall in the Alte Akademie Museum, home to the Bavarian State Collection of Paleontology and Historical Geology. In 1915, he also published a detailed scientific description of *Spinosaurus*, illustrated with meticulous figures depicting the bones he had found.

The size of Stromer's *Spinosaurus* eclipsed that of the more famous *Tyrannosaurus*, first described in 1905. *Spinosaurus* might have become one of the most familiar of all dinosaurs were it not for World War II. As fate would have it, the events of that war were to thrust Stromer's work into relative obscurity for many years. The fossils that represented his life's work—including *Spinosaurus*—were stored in the Alte Akademie Museum in Munich. On April 24, 1944, Britain and Germany were at war. The British Royal Air Force, while dropping bombs on a nearby military target, accidentally set fire to the museum housing Stromer's fossils. After the fire, all that remained of the spectacular *Spinosaurus* were Stromer's stories, field notes, and published descriptions.

For many years, Stromer's lost dinosaur was nearly forgotten. Fortunately, several discoveries since 1986—including those of *Baryonyx* (Early Cretaceous, England); *Suchomimus* (Early Cretaceous, Niger); and *Irritator* (Early Cretaceous, Brazil)—have revealed much more about the clade of dinosaurs to which *Spinosaurus* belonged. The spinosaurs not only had conical teeth similar to those of crocodiles, but also had skulls that were long and narrow and that featured a crocodilelike snout and a cluster of teeth at the front of the jaw. In the taxon *Suchomimus*, the bottom jaw has a rounded, chinlike "rosette" at its tip in which the largest teeth are housed. *Baryonyx* and *Suchomimus* also had powerful forelimbs and large claws on their hands; the longest of these claws was about 12 inches (30 cm) long. A combination of evidence—including their teeth, jaws, claws, and the sediments in which their remains are found—strongly suggests that the spinosaurs were fish eaters and used their powerful arms and claws to scoop fish from the water. The large sail-back found in *Spinosaurus* was not nearly as prominent in *Baryonyx* and *Suchomimus*.

Although Stromer's magnificent specimen of *Spinosaurus* was destroyed during World War II, the search for another specimen has been revived by a new generation of paleontologists. In 1999, armed only with Stromer's sketchy field notes, paleontologist Josh Smith and archaeologist Jennifer Smith visited Egypt in search of the famed fossil site. What they found during their quick foray were bone fragments strewn over the ground and enough evidence to compel them to return the following year. The subsequent expedition included teams from the University of Pennsylvania and Egyptian Geological Survey and Mining Authority headed by Josh Smith, Peter Dodson, Matthew Lamanna, and Yousry Attia.

The hardships of working in the desert had changed little since Stromer's time, but Smith and his team—unlike Stromer before them—were able to take up residence in a pleasant motel that served as their home for the duration of the dig. The team did not find another specimen of *Spinosaurus* apart from teeth, but it did make a major discovery of a sauropod from the time of *Spinosaurus*. *Paralititan*—or "tidal giant," after the coastal tidal environment in which the dinosaur once lived—is among the largest known sauropod dinosaurs, after only *Argentinosaurus*, *Puertasaurus*, and possibly *Sauroposeidon* and *Amphicoelias. Paralititan* was a heavy and stocky beast, about 80 to 100 feet (24 to 30 m) long and weighing as much as 50 tons (45 metric tons). *Paralititan* adds significantly to the legacy of Egyptian dinosaurs and the ecosystem once documented by Stromer.

Although the fossil-hunting team led by Josh Smith was unable to find a significant new specimen of *Spinosaurus*, its efforts have helped reinstate the gigantic theropod as a legitimate contender for the title of largest known predatory dinosaur. Nonetheless, additional hard evidence in the form of new fossil remains of *Spinosaurus* has been difficult to come by. In 1996, Canadian paleontologist Dale Russell (b. 1947) described fragmentary bones of *Spinosaurus* from Morocco including neck vertebrae, part of the spine, and pieces of the lower jaw. Other fragments have been reported from Tunisia and Algeria, but none of these specimens has significantly advanced knowledge of this enigmatic theropod. Even the rediscovery—in 2006, by Josh Smith and Matthew Lamanna—of two unpublished photographs of Stromer's *Spinosaurus* museum exhibit was an event, as the photographs provided long-unseen views of the original *Spinosaurus* specimen that was destroyed.

The most striking new fossil evidence for *Spinosaurus* was announced in 2005 by a multinational team of paleontologists led by Italian Cristiano Dal Sasso. This team had "rediscovered" a long-forgotten fossil fragment discovered in Morocco in 1975. The specimen is that of a remarkably preserved partial skull and upper jaw of *Spinosaurus*. The snout measures 3.25 feet (1 m) long, and the entire skull is estimated to have been 5.7 feet (1.7 m) long, the largest of any known spinosaur. The specimen is remarkably preserved in three dimensions—not squashed flat as can sometimes happen to bones during fossilization. The jaw includes many teeth that had not yet erupted to the surface.

Dal Sasso and his colleagues estimate that their specimen of *Spinosaurus* is about 20 percent larger than Stromer's. Using the body plan of *Suchomimus* as a guide to fill in the missing parts

Baryonyx and *Neovenator*, two large predatory dinosaurs from the Early Cretaceous of Great Britain

of the animal's body, this would make the Dal Sasso specimen of *Spinosaurus* 53 to 60 feet (16 to 18 m) long. This is 20 percent to 30 percent larger than *Baryonynx* and *Suchomimus* and even longer than *Tyrannosaurus* and *Giganotosaurus*, the two theropods most commonly assumed to be the largest. The table on the next page provides a comparison of the largest known theropods.

Avetheropoda

All tetanurans other than the Spinosauroidea were part of a group of related theropods named the Avetheropoda. The origins of this group date from the Middle Jurassic, and the group consisted of several diverse subgroups representing, among others, the smallest known dinosaurs as well as some of the largest. It is also within the Avetheropoda ("bird theropods") that the first definitive link between dinosaurs and modern birds is seen. In fact, the clade Avetheropoda was defined by American paleontologist Gregory Paul (b. 1954) in 1986 to include all advanced theropods encompassed by taxa such as *Allosaurus* and birds, a view that has been further reinforced since that time by a crush of new theropod discoveries, including feathered dinosaurs in China and new finds from the Southern Hemisphere. The Avetheropoda is defined as a taxon including *Allosaurus*, the modern house sparrow, their most

THE LARGEST PREDATORY DINOSAURS

Theropod name	Spinosaurus	Giganotosaurus	Mapusaurus	Carcharodontosaurus	Tyrannosaurus	Acrocanthosaurus
Phylogenetic affinity	Spinosaur	Carcharodontosaur	Carcharodontosaur	Carcharodontosaur	Tyrannosaur	Carcharodontosaur
Length	53 to 60 feet (16 to 18 m)	46 feet (13.7 m)	46 feet (13.7 m)	45 feet (13.5 m)	40 to 43 feet (12 to 13 m)	39 ft (12 m)
Weight	8 tons (7.2 tonnes)	7 tons (6.3 tonnes)	7 tons (6.3 tonnes)	7 tons (6.3 tonnes)	7 tons (6.3 tonnes)	5 tons (4.5 tonnes)
Location & time	North Africa, Late Cretaceous	Argentina, Late Cretaceous	Argentina, Late Cretaceous	North Africa, Late Cretaceous	North America, Argentina, Late Cretaceous	North America, Early Cretaceous
Distinctions	Sail-backed; conical teeth; fish eater	Longest known theropod skull (6.4 ft/1.9 m); bladelike teeth	Rivals its close cousin Giganotosaurus in size; bladelike teeth; deep skull	Bladelike teeth; skull length of 5.5 6 ft (1.6 m)	Short arms; two-clawed hands; banana-shaped teeth; skull length of 4.6 ft (1.4 m)	Largest North American theropod prior to tyrannosaurs

recent shared ancestor, and all of its descendants. The two major divisions found within the Avetheropoda, as discussed below, are the Carnosauria and Coelurosauria.

Carnosauria

The Carnosauria is a group of mostly large theropods measuring 16 feet (5 m) long or more and characterized by massive heads; burly, powerful necks; relatively short arms with three fingers per hand; powerful hind limbs; and long, deep tails. Except for the spinosaurs and tyrannosaurs, the largest theropods come from the ranks of the carnosaurs. Carnosauria includes three subgroups: the Sinraptoridae, the Allosauridae, and the Carcharodontosauridae.

The Sinraptoridae were large predators that measured up to 30 feet (9 m) long. Currently, the clade includes only two genera, both dating from the Late Jurassic of China: *Sinraptor* and *Yangchuanosaurus*. *Sinraptor* is the better known of these, with two species represented by nearly complete skulls and skeletons. Sinraptorids appear to be closely allied with allosaurids, with key differences being a longer and lower skull that is perforated with additional holes and a larger antorbital **fenestra,** or skull opening, in front of the eyes.

The clade Allosauridae was named after *Allosaurus* (Late Jurassic, western North America and Europe), one of the best known large theropods and one of only two taxa in this clade. *Allosaurus* was first discovered by fossil hunting crews working for Edward Drinker Cope in 1877, but Cope was delayed in examining the fossil, and the creature was subsequently named *Allosaurus* ("strange lizard") by Othniel Charles Marsh in the same year, based on a less impressive, fragmentary specimen. Many partial and complete skeletons and skulls of *Allosaurus* have since been found, making it one of the best-understood predatory dinosaurs.

Allosaurus was the most common large predator in North America during the Late Jurassic Epoch. Its large head, bladelike teeth, short arms with three-clawed hands, sturdy legs, and long tail characterize the basic traits of these carnosaurs. The *Allosaurus*

An *Allosaurus* skull

skull was also distinguished by a knobby horn on the brow above each eye. The largest allosaur specimens measure about 33 feet (10 m) long, big enough to threaten the well-being of the large herbivorous sauropods with which *Allosaurus* coexisted.

One of the most spectacular allosaur specimens is that of "Big Al," a subadult specimen discovered in Wyoming in 1991. This articulated skeleton was 95 percent complete and lay with its head twisted back in a convulsive death pose. Its excellent preservation is due to having been buried quickly by stream sediments that prevented the carcass from being scavenged by other animals.

Big Al was about 25 feet (7.5 m) long, making it nearly full grown. One remarkable aspect of the specimen is that the bones show evidence of a variety of life traumas and infections. At various points in its life, Big Al had broken several ribs and sustained injuries and infections to its hips, feet, and claws. Although the cause of these injuries cannot be known, it is not outside of the realm of possibility to think that this subadult had taken a beating while trying to attack a large sauropod and perhaps was brushed aside by a swipe of the herbivore's multi-ton tail. Whether these injuries led to the death of Big Al cannot be known, but the allosaur was certainly weaker and less able to defend itself while suffering from such maladies.

Recently, *Allosaurus* became one of the very few dinosaur genera known from more than one modern continent, with the discovery of *Allosaurus europaeus* in Portugal. Remains of this new European allosaurid include a nearly complete skull and some postcranial bones.

The only other taxon currently assigned to the Allosauridae is *Saurophaganax* (Late Jurassic, Oklahoma), based on a fragmentary specimen that may actually be a large specimen of *Allosaurus*. A few paleontologists also view *Acrocanthosaurus* (Early Cretaceous, Oklahoma and Texas) as an allosaurid, but most consider this taxon as part of the Carcharodontosauridae.

The third group of Carnosauria was the Carcharodontosauridae. During the Cretaceous, the Northern Hemisphere had Tyranno-saurus and its relatives; the Southern Hemisphere had the carcha-rodontosaurs. These extremely large-bodied predators arose in the Northern and Southern Hemispheres during the Early Cretaceous and were the dominant predators of their world until they dimin-ished early in the Late Cretaceous. Three of the six largest known theropods were carcharodontosaurs (see the table "The Largest Predatory Dinosaurs," page 67).

Ernst Stromer first proposed the clade of theropods known as Carcharodontosauridae in 1931; he based his proposal on the first specimen of *Carcharodontosaurus* (Late Cretaceous, Egypt), which he was the first to describe. The original specimen of *Carcharodon-tosaurus*, or "shark tooth lizard," consisted of fragmentary bones and teeth. Unfortunately, like the remains of *Spinosaurus*, the origi-nal specimen of *Carcharodontosaurus* was destroyed in a bombing run on Munich during World War II.

In 1995, Paul Sereno discovered an isolated but remarkably com-plete skull of *Carcharodontosaurus* in Morocco, thereby confirming its affinities within the Theropoda. Sereno and colleagues created the clade Carcharodontosauridae to include this dinosaur and other, similar giant predatory dinosaurs that have been found in the Southern Hemisphere. The Carcharodontosauridae are defined as consisting of *Carcharodontosaurus* and all species closer to *Carcharodontosaurus* than to either *Allosaurus, Sinraptor,* or the common house sparrow.

Carcharodontosaurus itself is best known from its enormous skull measuring 5.5 to 6 feet (1.6 to 2 m) long. The size of that skull has only now been eclipsed by that of the more recently discovered *Giganotosaurus,* a cousin from Argentina and also a carcharodontosaur.

Giganotosaurus (Late Cretaceous, Argentina), the "giant southern lizard," was described in 1995 by Argentinean paleontologists Rodolfo Coria and Leonardo Salgado and was immediately recognized as one of the largest known theropods, second only to the lost fossils of *Spinosaurus.* The original specimen was about 70 percent complete and represented a long, heavy-bodied predator measuring about 40 feet (12.2 m) long. In 1998, Jorge Orlando Calvo and Coria announced the discovery of a new specimen of *Giganotosaurus* with an isolated lower jaw, the size of which indicated an animal that was about 46 feet (13.7 m) long. *Giganotosaurus* had a large, long skull with a bony ridge running along the sides of the snout and short brow horns just before the eyes. Its jaw was lined with slender, bladelike teeth, the longest of which were about 6 inches (15 cm).

Unlike tyrannosaurs, whose jaw muscles ran further along the length of the jaw to provide increased bite force, the muscles of the *Giganotosaurus* jaw and those of other carcharodontosaurs were largely concentrated at the rear of the jaw to improve the speed with which the dinosaurs could snap their jaws onto their prey. *Giganotosaurus* and other carcharodontosaurs probably used a grapple-and-bite killing tactic: They probably used their hand claws to hold or bring down the prey while their teeth did the killing. The narrow, bladelike teeth of carcharodontosaurs were well adapted for ripping ribbons of flesh from their victims.

Mapusaurus (Late Cretaceous, Argentina) is another carcharodontosaur of immense size like that of its close relative, *Giganotosaurus.*

The largest known specimen of *Mapusaurus* would have been about 41 feet (12.2 m) long. The skull of *Mapusaurus* differed significantly from that of *Giganotosaurus* by having a shorter snout; a narrower shape; a relatively large, triangular-shaped skull opening in front of the eyes; and a bumpy ridge extending on both sides of the skull from just behind the nostril, over the brow, and behind the eye.

Perhaps the most remarkable part of the *Mapusaurus* story is that the animal's discovery included the recovery of individuals of different ages from the same **bone bed**. The specimens ranged in size from 17 to 41 feet (5 to 12.2 m). The excavation and description of *Mapusaurus* was a joint effort by the Argentinean-Canadian Dinosaur Project led by Rodolfo Coria and Canadian Phil Currie. The job of excavating such a rich deposit of fossils required five field seasons between 1997 and 2001.

Having been a crew member for the 1999 expedition, I can attest to the enormous amount of work required simply to expose the bone bed so that the careful work of extracting bones could begin in earnest. The first week was spent chipping away with shovels, picks, chisels, and hammers at the massive amount of rock, called overburden, that covered most of the site. The crew removed an estimated 15 to 20 tons (14 to 18 tonnes) of rock over the course of a week—enough to fill a few small trucks. All of this was done using hand tools and plastic buckets to carry the rock to a waste pile. Removing the hundreds of bones required part of the 1999 field season plus two more.

The bone bed itself is interpreted as a freshwater deposit, probably formed by seasonally heavy rains in an arid or semiarid climate. Although the bone bed might represent a long-term accumulation of individual carcasses, the occurrence strongly suggests that a group of large theropods traveling together might have perished at the same time. This is unusual in the study of theropods because the remains of most predatory dinosaurs are found in isolation. It is generally assumed that they hunted alone.

Evidence that some of the largest of the theropods may have traveled in groups is extremely rare. A site in western Canada contains fossils of 22 individuals of the tyrannosaur *Albertosaurus* (Late

Cretaceous) that perished suddenly. The group consisted of juveniles and adults and is considered by paleontologist Phil Currie to have been a hunting pack. In imagining their behavior, Currie suggested that the swifter juveniles might have gone ahead of the pack to chase down and trouble a prey group, such as hadrosaurs. They would eventually single out individuals and distract them until the adults could arrive to make the kill. Currie later revised this view in 2006, saying that it was also feasible that the group was merely an accumulation of individuals rather than a pack, although evidence of group behavior in large theropods from other localities continues to fuel speculation about pack behavior in the biggest meat-eaters.

The *Mapusaurus* site also contains individuals of various sizes, from juvenile to adult, and suggests that they were traveling in a group when overcome by a violent rush of floodwater. If this group

THINK ABOUT IT

The Worldwide Distribution of Dinosaurs

The subject of bias in the fossil record was discussed in Chapter 2. One factor affecting the discovery of fossils is whether the proper sedimentary layers of the Earth are accessible to people who are looking for fossils. Earth's crust is a moveable layer that consists of tectonic plates. Geologic forces slowly change the surface of the Earth by pushing these plates together, folding them over and under themselves, raising older layers to the surface, and pushing more recent layers down below. As a result, some ancient layers containing dinosaur fossils that have been buried by millions of years of sedimentation find their way to the surface, where erosion can expose evidence of ancient life.

Just where such fossil exposures are located is key to the success of paleontology. Relying on geologic maps that have been created during the past 200 years, paleontologists seek areas to explore that are likely to contain sedimentary rocks—and, hopefully, fossils—from the span of time that interests them.

was a hunting pack, it is conceivable that these large predators worked together to bring down such gigantic prey as the sauropod *Argentinosaurus*, which also lived in the area at the same time.

Coelurosauria

The Coelurosauria represent a widely diverse group of theropods ranging in size from the tiny *Microraptor* and *Compsognathus* to the enormous *Tyrannosaurus*. The name Coelurosauria means "hollow-tail lizards." When the name was proposed in 1920, the group was intended to include mostly small predatory dinosaurs that had lightweight skeletal features. The category became a dumping ground for many difficult-to-classify theropod taxa that were not part of a naturally related group.

The Coelurosauria was recently redefined by French paleontologist Jacques Gauthier and others as a key subgroup within the Avetheropoda. The group Coelurosauria is divided into four main groups and then several subgroups—the Compsognathidae, Tyrannosauroidea, Ornithomimosauria, Therizinosauridae, and Maniraptora. The subgroup Maniraptora, in turn, is further divided into several lines of small- to medium-sized non-avian theropods, plus the basal birds. The origin of birds will be discussed in more detail in Chapter 4.

The coelurosaurs represented the final great radiation and evolution of non-avian theropods before their demise at the end of the Late Cretaceous Epoch. As such, coelurosaurs are the most derived (i.e. birdlike) versions of several lines of theropods and represent the extreme trends that were taking place just before the end-Cretaceous mass extinction.

Compsognathidae

The compsognathids ("delicate jaws") were small basal coelurosaurs with birdlike bodies. Only a few taxa currently make up this group; they lived during the Late Jurassic of Germany and France and the Early Cretaceous of England, China, and Brazil. *Compsognathus* (Late Jurassic, Germany and France) was discovered in 1861 in the same quarries as *Archaeopteryx* and was in some ways similar to

Sinornithosaurus had teeth that were characteristic of dinosaurs but not true birds.

this early bird, with a long neck, a tail, and long legs, but not wings or feathers. *Compsognathus* is known only from two specimens and for many years languished as a mysterious taxon without any obvious closely related kin. A discovery in China in 1995 was to change the status of *Compsognathus* considerably, however.

In the 1990s, a stream of fossils dating from the Early Cretaceous of northeastern China began to emerge from the province of Liaoning. Among the first to appear was a slab of mudstone with the flattened remains of a small predatory dinosaur. The skeleton of this creature was remarkably well preserved in much the same manner as that of the famous *Archaeopteryx*. The tiniest of details were visible. The dinosaur measured only 3.3 feet (1 m) long and was complete except for the tip of its tail. With its meat-eating teeth, short arms, and long legs, it looked much like *Compsognathus*. Most exciting, however, was that the skeleton was outlined with the texture of filaments of fuzz, or "protofeathers," which could be likened to the downy coating seen on modern birds before they reach maturity and grow true feathers. The new dinosaur was named *Sinosauropteryx* ("Chinese lizard wing") by Chinese scientists and soon joined *Compsognathus* as one of the primitive members of a clade that preceded an explosion of feathered dinosaur and bird evolution in the Early and Late Cretaceous Epochs.

Tyrannosauroidea

Tyrannosaurs were once categorized as members of the Carnosauria because of their large size and superficial similarity to carnosaurs such as *Allosaurus*; however, closer examination by American paleontologist Thomas Holtz in 1994 revealed some derived traits of the foot that tyrannosaurs shared with coelurosaurs, including the ornithomimosaurs and troodontids. Resurrecting an old hypothesis first postulated by the legendary German paleontologist Friedrich von Huene (1875–1969), Holtz's well-reasoned and exacting analysis resulted in a major redefinition of tyrannosaurs and their place in the evolutionary tree of dinosaurs. Rather than being closely related to such early large predators as *Allosaurus*, *T. rex* and its kin were actually an extraordinary branch of the same dinosaur lineage that gave us birds. The subsequent discovery of earlier and smaller members of the tyrannosaur line has firmly rooted Holtz's view of tyrannosaur evolution and helped better define coelurosaurs as a natural group of related organisms.

Tyrannosaurs are known for several features unique to their clade. Their broad, massive skulls were supported by short, powerful necks. Unlike the bladelike teeth of most theropods, the teeth at the tip of the tyrannosaurs' upper jaw were shaped like a "D" in cross-section, and in derived tyrannosaurids, the teeth were thick and banana-shaped, with sharp serrations and deep roots. This gave these predators the ability to bite and crush bone with their powerful jaws. Tyrannosaur heads were massive and seemingly oversized in proportion to their stout bodies. The tyrannosaur forelimbs were short and strong and had only two digits—a derived trait not seen in other theropod clades.

The roots of the Tyrannosauroidea tree began with much smaller coelurosaurs that arose in the Late Jurassic Epoch. The traits that link them to *T. rex* are limited at first to certain features of the skull. The earliest known relative of the tyrannosaurs was *Guanlong,* from the Late Jurassic of China. It lived 160 million years ago, which was before *Archaeopteryx* and other known feathered dinosaurs and early birds, but could be related to the line of theropods that led to *Tyrannosaurus* some 90 million years later. *Guanlong* was not the top predator of its day, measuring only about 10 feet (3 m) long, a far cry from the 43-foot (13 m), 7-ton (6.3 metric ton) behemoth that was *Tyrannosaurus. Guanlong,* whose name means "crowned dragon," was described in 2006 by a team led by Xing Xu of the Institute of Vertebrate Paleontology and Paleoanthropology in Beijing. The name is a tip of the hat to *Tyrannosaurus rex,* the "tyrant lizard king," but also refers to an unusual and prominent oval-shaped nasal crest that sits atop the centerline of the skull. The relationship of *Guanlong* to tyrannosaurs is not obvious to the casual observer. Among the major differences were its small size, head crest, long arms, and three claws on each hand—not two claws as known for later tyrannosaurs. Examination of the skull openings and teeth, however, reveals close affinities with tyrannosaurids, so it would appear that the evolution of coelurosaurs in the direction of *Tyrannosaurus* began in the skull.

The next important link in the evolution of tyrannosaurs was another Asian theropod named *Dilong* (Early Cretaceous, China), or "emperor dragon," described in 2004 by Xing Xu and colleagues. Dating from 128 million years ago, *Dilong* was discovered in the fossil-rich deposits of Liaoning in northeastern China. At only about 5 feet (1.5 m) long, this lightly built theropod was also far smaller than *T. rex,* but it shared traits of the skull and teeth, thus linking it to tyrannosaurids.

Specimens of *Dilong* also show that it was cloaked in *Sinosauropteryx*-like "protofeathers," a trait that insulated its body and that was unrelated to flight (see Chapter 4). *Dilong* also had three digits on its hands, not two as in the later, large-bodied tyrannosaurs. The presence of protofeathers in *Dilong* suggests that all tyrannosaurs—even the mighty *T. rex*—may have been feathered at some stage of their lives. Because feathers in non-avian dinosaurs would have been used primarily for insulation, display, or gliding, larger tyrannosaurs were probably only feathered as hatchlings or juveniles. Upon reaching maturity, their body size probably would have been sufficient to retain enough heat to maintain their thermo-regulatory requirements.

The Asian localities of *Guanlong* and *Dilong* suggest that early tyrannosaurs may have originated there, but several other specimens of proposed early tyrannosaurs, most of which are fragmentary or of questionable affiliation, hail from the Late Jurassic of England (*Iliosuchus*); Portugal (*Aviatyrannis*); and Utah (*Stokesosaurus*); and from the Early Cretaceous of England (*Eotyrannus*). Even when *Guanlong* and *Dilong* are taken into account, there remains a considerable gap in the evolutionary record of tyrannosaurs leading to the Late Cretaceous appearance of *Tyrannosaurus* (Late Cretaceous, western North America) and its close relatives.

Tyrannosaurus was the largest predatory dinosaur in the Northern Hemisphere during the Late Cretaceous. Its highly derived adaptations veered somewhat away from the body plan found in most other theropods. It had extremely short but muscular arms with only two claws per hand. Its teeth were thick and chunky and its head wide, bulky, and heavily muscled in a way that optimized its jaws for biting down firmly with great force. Unlike the carcharodontosaurid giants of the Southern Hemisphere, which used their bladelike teeth to slice away at the flesh of prey, tyrannosaurs were built for brute force. Tyrannosaurs were likely pursue-and-bite predators, taking advantage of their long legs, huge raptorial feet, muscular necks, and jaws lined with sturdy, bone-crunching teeth. After chasing down their prey, tyrannosaurs probably completed the kill using a combination of biting to the neck or clamping down on the muzzle of the prey, each of which could result in mortal injury or suffocation. Their foot claws were used to hold down the prey rather than to slash them. Tyrannosaurs probably fed by clamping

Tyrannosaurus rex

down on the body with their jaws, then pulling and twisting with their enormous strength to rip chunks of meat from their prey.

Tyrannosaurus is the largest and best-known tyrannosaur. It had smaller close relatives in the Late Cretaceous of Asia and western and eastern North America, including *Albertosaurus* (Alberta and

Montana); *Daspletosaurus* (Alberta and Montana); *Gorgosaurus* (Alberta); *Appalachiosaurus* (Alabama); *Alectrosaurus* (Mongolia and China); *Alioramus* (Mongolia); *Tarbosaurus* (Mongolia and China); and possibly *Dryptosaurus* (New Jersey).

Ornithomimosauria

Ornithomimosaurs ("bird mimic lizards") bore a striking, although superficial, resemblance to modern-day ostriches and other large, flightless ground birds. Although they are not closely related to ostriches, ornithomimosaurs had a similar body plan, with long legs for running and a long, S-curved neck with a small head, the latter typically equipped with a toothless beak. Ornithomimosaurs were among the fastest of dinosaurs. Estimated top speeds for ornithomimosaurs range from 30 to 50 mph (50 to 80 km/h). They had long, slender arms and hands equipped with three sicklelike claws for defending from predators or possibly grasping prey. The most basal members of this clade had small teeth, a feature missing from more derived taxa in favor of toothless beaks. The group Ornithomimosauria is divided into three subgroups: the Harpymimidae, the Deinocheiridae, and the Ornithomimidae.

Pelecanimimus ("pelican mimic"), from the Early Cretaceous of Spain, is the oldest and most basal ornithomimosaur currently known. It is represented by an excellent specimen consisting of the front half of the skeleton, but no legs. *Pelecanimimus* was small, measuring only about 6 to 8 feet (1.8 to 2.5 m) long. Its skull was long and low, and its jaws contained an enormous number of teeth—especially considering that most other members of this line of theropods were toothless. Surprisingly, *Pelecanimimus* had about 220 teeth, more than half of which were found closely packed in the dentary (the forward-most bone of the lower jaw). The premaxilla and **maxilla** (upper jaw) had teeth only in the forward part of the mouth, followed by bony ridges instead of teeth to complete the upper biting surfaces. This is remarkable, considering that the next-oldest basal ornithomimosaurs, *Harpymimus* (Early Cretaceous, Mongolia) and *Shenzhousaurus* (Early Cretaceous, China), had only 10 or 11 and

7 or 8 teeth, respectively, and these were found only in the dentary. In most other respects, *Pelecanimimus*, *Harpymimus*, and *Shenzhousaurus* resemble smaller versions of later ornithomimosaurs.

Having evolved from earlier lines of tooth-bearing predatory dinosaurs, it was assumed that ornithomimosaurs acquired their toothless condition through the gradual reduction of the number of teeth over time. *Harpymimus*, discovered in 1984, did much to support this idea. The discovery of *Pelecanimimus*, a geologically earlier taxon than *Harpymimus*, suggested otherwise. When *Pelecanimimus* was first described in 1994 by Spanish paleontologist B.P. Pérez-Moreno and colleagues, they needed to reverse some established logic about the progression from teeth to beaks in ornithomimosaurs. Pérez-Moreno reasoned that closely packed teeth could have become increasingly fused over many generations, effectively creating a cutting and ripping surface analogous to that of a toothless beak. *Harpymimus* and *Shenzhousaurus* might represent theropods in the middle of such an evolutionary transition, having already adapted to a closely fused cutting edge.

The subgroup Deinocheiridae is represented by only one highly enigmatic taxon, Deinocheirus ("terrible hand"), from the Late Cretaceous of Mongolia. The only known specimen of this theropod consists of a pair of long, robust forelimbs that measure about 8 feet (2.5 m) long and are adorned with massive, 10-inch (25 cm) claws, plus some fragments of ribs and vertebrae. The arms most closely resemble those of other ornithomimosaurs—hence the current association of *Deinocheirus* with this clade. If this dinosaur was indeed an ornithomimosaur, the length of the forelimbs suggests that the entire animal could have been between 25 and 35 feet (8 and 11 m) long.

The subgroup Ornithomimidae includes the best-known and most derived ornithomimosaurs. All of these taxa are found in the Northern Hemisphere, as are all known basal ornithomimosaurs, and hail from either Asia or western North America. Two of the most studied taxa are *Gallimimus* (Late Cretaceous, Mongolia) and *Struthiomimus* (Late Cretaceous, Alberta and Montana).

Gallimimus ("chicken mimic") was described by Mongolian paleontologist Rinchen Barsbold and Polish paleontologists Halszka Osmólska and Ewa Roniewicz in 1972. It is known from several specimens ranging in size from juvenile to adult. The largest known specimen of *Gallimimus* reached 13 to 20 feet (4 to 6 m) in length and may have stood about 6 feet (2 m) tall at the hip. *Gallimimus* had legs especially well adapted for running and a long tail that served as a counterbalance while it ran. Its skull was long, with large eyes and a toothless, almost ducklike beak.

Struthiomimus was discovered in 1914 and first described by Henry Fairfield Osborn (1857–1935) of the American Museum of Natural History. *Struthiomimus* represents the first well-understood ornithomimosaur. Measuring between 10 and 13 feet (3 to 4 m) long, this ornithomimosaur had the characteric slender forelimbs, grasping claws, and small, ostrichlike head associated with other members of this clade.

The toothless beak of ornithomimosaurs has been a source of much speculation regarding the diet of these theropods. As early as 1917, Osborn suggested that these dinosaurs subsisted on an herbivorous diet of soft shoots and buds from plants. Evidence of gastroliths found with several ornithimimosaur specimens supports this hypothesis because stomach stones are used by some herbivorous dinosaurs to help pulverize tough plant material. This would not have precluded ornithomimosaurs from also eating small vertebrates such as lizards or small birds as well as insects. As such, ornithomimosaurs represent a branch of the theropod evolutionary tree that may have been **omnivorous**. The recent discovery of evidence of soft-tissue structures in the beaks of two ornithomimosaur specimens also suggests that some specimens may have used their beaks to strain food particles from water in streams and lakes.

Maniraptora

Maniraptora is a natural group of related theropods that includes the evolutionary stock from which birds arose. This is not to say that all maniraptorans were small or birdlike. Members of this

clade vary considerably in their outward appearance and size, ranging from small to medium-sized theropods. Anatomical traits that
unite maniraptorans include modifications to the wrist and forelimbs that made grasping and twisting of the hand possible and led
to the flight stroke in birds; a clavicle, or "wishbone," in the collar
area; a downward- or backward-pointing **pubis** bone in the pelvis
(most saurischians had a forward-pointing pubis); a shortened tail
that was stiff at the distal (outer) end; long arms; and a three-clawed
hand that was larger than the foot. There is growing evidence that
all subgroups within Maniraptora had feathers. Maniraptorans are
divided into five subgroups: the Oviraptorosauria, Troodontidae,
Therizinosauroidea, Alvarezsauridae, and Dromaeosauridae.

The Oviraptorosauria included theropods that measured from
a modest 6.6 feet (2 m) to 27 feet (8 m) long and that currently are
known with certainty only from the Northern Hemisphere. Known
from 20 or more taxa, the oviraptorosaur body is similar to that of
other small theropods and has the long, slender arms and grasping
claws of other maniraptorans. Some members of the group—such as
Oviraptor, *Rinchenia*, and *Citipati*, all from the Late Cretaceous of
Mongolia—had large crests at the front of the skull, extending from
the nasal bones. The *Oviraptor* skull is unique among dinosaurs
and quite alien in appearance, even among theropods. The skull
was tall with a short snout and large, toothless beak. The purpose
of the large nasal crest is not entirely understood, but in addition to
providing a visual display, it may have been adapted for the purpose
of making sound and possibly to enable the dinosaur to absorb more
moisture from the warm air of its arid environment.

The toothless beak of most oviraptorosaurs was part of a
strong, muscular jaw. Without teeth, one might assume that these
oviraptorosaurs were either insectivores or herbivores, and it would
appear that they were well adapted for a variety of foods. Their jaws
could have been used to crack open clams and mollusks that lived in
freshwater streams and lakes in their habitat. The powerful grasping
claws of oviraptorosaurs strongly suggest that they also may have
fed on small vertebrates—such as frogs, lizards, snakes, birds, and

mammals—which they could snatch up and dispatch with a crushing bite.

The first described member of the Oviraptorosauria was *Oviraptor*, discovered in Mongolia by famed fossil hunter Roy Chapman Andrews (1884–1960) and his team, working for the American Museum of Natural History. Andrews had found the remains of the little theropod in the midst of a nest of dinosaur eggs. Because abundant adult fossils of the horned dinosaur *Protoceratops* had also been found in the vicinity, it was assumed by paleontologist Henry Fairfield Osborn, who first provided a scientific description of *Oviraptor*, that the predator was plundering a nest of *Protoceratops* at the time of its untimely demise. Hence the name *Oviraptor philoceratops*—"egg stealer fond of ceratopsians."

Years later, in 1994, Mark Norell (b. 1957) and colleagues, also of the American Museum of Natural History, announced the discovery of an *Oviraptor* embryo within one of the very kinds of eggs that were once thought to have been those of the horned dinosaur *Protoceratops*. Soon after correcting this case of mistaken identity, at least two additional oviraptorosaur fossil specimens of *Citipati* were discovered in which an adult individual was sitting atop a nest of its own eggs, apparently brooding in the manner of modern birds. This is one of the strongest cases from the fossil record of dinosaurs that at least some taxa engaged in some degree of parental care over their unhatched eggs.

One of the most primitive or basal oviraptorosaurs was *Caudipteryx* (Early Cretaceous, China), a remarkable creature known from at least nine nearly complete specimens. *Caudipteryx* comes from the same fossil deposits in the Liaoning region of northeastern China that is now famous for a variety of vertebrate, invertebrate, and plant fossils, including many birds and feathered dinosaurs.

Described in 1998 by paleontologists Qiang Ji, Phil Currie, Mark Norell, and others, *Caudipteryx* provided the first definitive evidence of modern birdlike feathers on a non-avian theropod. Close study showed that its jaw was nearly toothless except for four premaxillary teeth; this suggested that it and other basal oviraptorosaurs, including *Avimimus* and *Incisivosaurus,* were evolving in the direction of a toothless beak, as seen in later members of this group. *Caudipteryx* was between 3 and 4 feet (1 m) long. Its arms were short, its neck was long, and its hind legs were long and suited for running. Impressions of feathers found with the skeletal elements show that *Caudipteryx* had short, downy feathers covering its body, plus a tuft of longer feathers on its forelimbs and a fanlike spread of feathers on its short tail. The feathers were short and similar to those seen in modern flightless birds. Several specimens of *Caudipteryx* have been found with a collection of gastroliths in the abdominal region, suggesting that this animal may have been an herbivore with a gizzard similar to modern birds.

Another important oviraptorosaur specimen is that of *Nomingia* (Late Cretaceous, Mongolia). Although consisting of only a partial postcranial skeleton, this specimen is significant because the blunt tail of this oviraptorosaur ended with several short, fused vertebrae, a feature interpreted by some paleontologists as that of a **pygostyle**. In birds, the pygostyle is a place of attachment for the tail feathers. Moreover, an as yet-undescribed caenagnathid at the Carnegie Museum in Pittsburgh includes a tail tipped by several very short, interlocking vertebrae that, when articulated, resemble a pygostyle, although because they're not fused together they cannot really be considered one.

The maniraptorans known as the Troodontidae make up a small clan known from 10 taxa found in western North America, Uzbekistan, Mongolia, and China. Dating from the Early Cretaceous Epoch, troodontids were lightly built theropods that measured no more than 6.5 feet (2 m) long. Their anatomy speaks to an active predatory lifestyle: long arms with raptorial hand claws, long legs for running, and a mouth full of small, recurved, serrated teeth seen in some species. Of all the dinosaurs, troodontids possessed some of the largest brains relative to body size, which extended their sensorial acuteness beyond that seen in most other theropods. Troodontids are known for having large eyes and probably also had excellent hearing. These sensory advantages, combined with their lightly built anatomy, suggest that troodontids were active and agile predators.

The fossil record of troodontids is spotty. The best-known taxon, *Troodon* ("wounding tooth"), is known from at least 20 partial specimens found in such localities as Montana, Alberta, Wyoming, and Mexico. The animal was originally named by American pale-ontologist Joseph Leidy (1823–1891) in 1856, based only on a tooth. The best-understood skull of a troodontid is that of *Saurornithoides* (Late Cretaceous, Mongolia), for which both an adult and juvenile specimen are known. *Byronosaurus*, *Mei*, *Jinfengopteryx*, and *Sinornithoides* (Early to Late Cretaceous, Mongolia and China) are also known from complete or nearly complete skulls.

The troodontids possessed another anatomical feature seen in a related group of maniraptorans: a deadly, sicklelike claw on the second toe of each foot that could be raised off the ground while the animal walked or ran. This claw was probably used for attacking prey and became a larger and more lethal weapon in the Dromaeosauridae.

The therizinosaurs represent another branch of theropods that adapted to eating plants. The bizarre morphology of this group is accented by the enormous, scythelike claws on their forelimbs, a distinctive feature that inspired the name therizinosaur, which means "reaping lizard." Therizinosaurs have been found in Northern Hemisphere outcrops dating from the Early to Late Cretaceous in North America and Asia. As a subgroup within the Coelurosauria, therizinoaurs are defined as all taxa representing the last common ancestor of *Therizinosaurus* (the most derived member) and *Beipiaosaurus* (the least derived member) and all of its descendants. There are currently 12 recognized taxa of therizinosaurs.

The therizinosaur body plan was that of a rotund body with wide hips, a long neck, a small head, and long arms with sicklelike claws. The animals were small to large-sized theropods that evolved from small, goose-sized taxa to monstrous, overgrown turkeylike creatures that may have measured up to 33 feet (10 m) long or more.

The long necks, leaf-shaped teeth, bipedal posture, and four-toed hind limbs of therizinosaurs invite comparisons with prosauropods. Like prosauropods and ornithomimosaurs, the most derived therizinosaurs were probably vegetarian and used their long necks to reach high into trees to grasp leaves. They possibly used their clawed hands to shovel branches into their mouths, where their teeth could strip off the leaves and buds. For many years, the remains of known therizinosaurs were scant and partial, leaving much guesswork as to their true evolutionary affinity within the dinosaurs. With nothing more to go by, the anatomical traits of therizinosaurs appeared to mix features of prosauropods, ornithischians, and theropods, creating a confusing picture.

The description of *Beipiaosaurus* (Early Cretaceous, China) in 1999 added much to the knowledge of therizinosaurs. This early, small therizinosaur measured about 7 feet (2.2 m) long and was the most complete therizinosaur found to date. This dinosaur had a bony beak and cheek teeth, an early adaptation toward more efficient plant eating. It also had three functional, weight-supporting toes—not four like the later therizinosaurs. This suggests that the four-toed foot was derived by therizinosaurs on their own and not inherited from a prosauropod ancestor. As if to dramatize the theropod link even more, *Beipiaosaurus* was covered with a bushy coat of feathers, further linking it to Maniraptorans and other non-avian dinosaurian relatives of birds. The anatomical affinities of therizinosaurs are so close to those of maniraptorans that many cladistic studies now place the clade Therizinosauroidea within the Maniraptora.

An important basal therizinosaur was *Falcarius* (Early Cretaceous, Utah). Measuring up to 13 feet (4 m) long, this medium-sized theropod is known from an abundance of fossil specimens recently discovered in Utah and described by paleontologist James Kirkland (b. 1954) and his colleagues. Kirkland says that literally thousands of disarticulated specimens of *Falcarius* have been found in two adjacent Utah sites, apparently drowned by a flood as the dinosaurs gathered or migrated as a large group. It will take many years for paleontologists to fully comprehend the amount of information available from a site of these extraordinary proporations. Even during the early stages of analysis, however, it appears that *Falcarius* may fill an important evolutionary gap between earlier carnivorous coelurosaurs and the later herbivorous therizinosaurs. Several adaptations seen in *Falcarius* make this evident, including the development of leaf-shaped teeth similar to those that evolved separately in sauropods, a bony beak at the front of the mouth, and expansion of the pelvic region to accommodate greater intestinal volume.

Therizinosaurus (Late Cretaceous, Mongolia) was one of the last and most derived members of the clade. Discovered in fragmentary pieces over the course of several fossil-hunting expeditions by a joint team of Soviet and Mongolian paleontologists, it was officially described by Russian E.A. Maleev in 1954. Still, the *Therizinosaurus* specimen consisted only of elements of the forelimb and possibly the hind limb, so the precise nature of the animal remained largely unknown until fossils of other therizinosaurs came to light. Descriptions of *Erlikosaurus* and *Segnosaurus*, both from the Late Cretaceous of Mongolia, emerged between 1979 and 1981, revealing detail about the skulls, teeth, and postcranial skeletons of therizinosaurs.

In addition to the discoveries of the early therizinosaurs *Beipiaosaurus* and *Falcarius*, knowledge about the later therizinosaurs has grown considerably because of several discoveries beyond the provenance of Mongolia. *Nothronychus* (Late Cretaceous, New Mexico) included a fragmentary but informative partial skeleton and skull. *Erlianosaurus* and *Neimongosaurus*, both from the Late Cretaceous of China, were important to understanding the spinal, limb, and pelvic elements of this clade.

The Alvarezsauridae include five known taxa of enigmatic theropods from the Early and Late Cretaceous of Argentina and Mongolia that may be more closely related to non-avian theropods than to birds. As these creatures have come to light only since the 1991 description of *Alvarezsaurus* (Late Cretaceous, Argentina), not enough is yet known about them to fully understand their evolutionary relationship to true birds. Alvarezsaurids were small;

they were no more than 6.6 feet (2 m) long. They had tiny teeth, long and narrow snouts, and extremely short forelimbs with a single, pronounced claw each. Alvarezsaurids were flightless.

Shuvuuia (Late Cretaceous, Argentina) and *Mononykus* (Late Cretaceous, Mongolia) are the two best-known specimens. The only good specimen of an alvarezsaurid skull is that of *Shuvuuia;* it was long and slender and had an upper jaw that was hinged at the point where it connected to the skull, thus providing great flex. This was a feature found in later birds but not found in other non-avian dinosaurs. The specimen of *Shuvuuia* also showed evidence of a downy covering of protofeathers. The relationship of alvarezsaurids to other non-avian theropods is clouded by the fact that the alvarezsaurids' single-clawed, stubby forelimb adaptation is unlike that of either maniraptoran dinosaurs or birds. These theropods could not fly, but there is evidence yet to be clarified that might reveal whether they evolved from earlier flying ancestors or from non-avian theropods.

In a category of its own is another early bird named *Rahonavis,* from the Late Cretaceous of Madagascar. The evolutionary affinities of this theropod are not entirely certain. When it was first described, by paleontologist Catherine Forster and her colleagues, *Rahonavis* ("menace from the clouds bird") was believed to be a primitive bird with close ties to the dromaeosaurid dinosaurs; like them, *Rahonavis* included a large, curved claw on the second toe of the foot. About the size of *Archaeopteryx*, *Rahonavis* was certainly a predatory creature with dinosaur roots, but the viability of its wings was questioned. Along with *Shuvuuia* and *Mononykus*, which also had close ties to birds but could not fly, *Rahonavis* suggests that some theropods may have become birds and then secondarily lost the ability to fly in later generations.

All of these specimens date from the end of the Cretaceous, some 75 million years or more after the first bird, *Archaeopteryx*. Such enigmas illustrate that fossils provide an incomplete picture of the true diversity of past life, and that evolution is capable of going in many directions at the same time, as dictated by the habitat and succession of traits that inhabit a given taxa. By the end of the Cretaceous, Madagascar was separated from the landmass that now forms India. The isolation of *Rahonavis* and other dinosaurs on this island during the Late Cretaceous may have resulted in some highly specialized adaptations not seen in other parts of the world. The Dromaeosauridae, known to many members of the public as "raptors," were small to medium-sized predators that are the closest known relatives of birds, making their anatomy of special significance to paleontologists interested in understanding the evolutionary relationship between dinosaurs and birds. Dromaeosaurs ("swift lizards") were bipedal with three weight-supporting toes on the feet that included a large, recurved, and retractable killing claw on the inner toe. Their forelimbs were long with flexible wrists and grasping hands that had three fingers with pronounced, sicklelike claws. The dromaeosaur tail was long and greatly stiffened, probably for improved balance and maneuverability. Their skulls were generally slim and light. Their teeth were fairly uniform in size, bladelike, and serrated, and included four somewhat less curved teeth in the front of the upper jaw. The smallest known dromaeosaur is also one of the smallest known dinosaurs: the birdlike *Microraptor* (Early Cretaceous, China) was a mere 2.5 feet (76 cm) long. The largest known raptors are known only from partial specimens. *Achillobator* (Late Cretaceous, Mongolia) was up to 20 feet (6 m) long and *Utahraptor* (Early Cretaceous, Utah) was about 23 feet (7 m) long and had an enormous foot claw measuring 9 inches (23 cm). Eleven taxa of dromaeosaurs are currently known from decent fossil evidence.

The first dromaeosaur described was *Dromaeosaurus* (Late Cretaceous, Alberta), but was known only from an incomplete skull and a few other bones. The importance of dromaeosaurs in understanding the evolution and biology of dinosaurs took on much greater significance with the discovery of *Deinonychus* in Montana in the late 1960s. Described by paleontologist John Ostrom in 1969, *Deinonychus* became one of the best-known dromaeosaur taxa and ignited modern debates about the lifestyle and metabolism of theropods as well as the evolutionary link between dromaeosaurs and birds. *Deinonychus* was a slender but powerful theropod measuring about 10 feet (3 m) long.

Deinonychus provided the first fairly complete picture of a dromaeosaur, and Ostrom quickly recognized its significance for the evolutionary history of theropods. He was struck by the similarities between *Deinonychus* and *Archaeopteryx*, the first bird, and detailed many anatomical similarities between the two. It was Ostrom's conclusion that dromaeosaurs and *Archaeopteryx* both evolved from a common ancestor—probably a small, bipedal, predatory dinosaur from the Early or Middle Jurassic. By the time of *Archaeopteryx* in the Late Jurassic Epoch, early birds had begun to evolve separately from their non-flying theropod relatives, the dromaeosaurs. Whether *Archaeopteryx* was an important link in this chain or merely an evolutionary dead end has yet to be proven. Likewise, the search continues for a common ancestor of both birds and dromaeosaurs from fossil deposits of Middle Jurassic age.

In addition to its anatomical links to birds, Ostrom also revived the debate over the lifestyle of theropods. What he saw in the anatomy of *Deinonychus* was an agile, alert, and quick-moving predator. The quarry in which the original specimens of *Deinonychus* were found contained several individuals of this theropod as well as a skeleton of the larger herbivorous dinosaur *Tenontosaurus*. Ostrom interpreted this as suggesting that *Deinonychus* hunted in packs, an activity requiring intra-species coordination and communication. In his view, it was incorrect to picture all dinosaurs as being passive, stupid, and slow-moving. It seemed that at least some species, such as *Deinonychus*, were active and possibly endothermic, two ideas that have since become accepted once again by most specialists in the field.

The retractable claw on the foot of dromaeosaurs was a remarkable adaptation. It was probably used to slash the prey—either to disembowel them outright or to weaken them through blood loss—or to pin down small prey. When not in use, the claw could be neatly raised out of the way so that the predator could walk or run without being inhibited. When brought into play during an attack, the claw was leveraged perfectly with the force of the leg to deliver maximum power to the point of contact, digging deep into the prey if the dromaeosaur was able to put its weight behind it.

Microraptor

At least two genera of early dromaeosaurs, *Microraptor* and *Sinornithosaurus*, show clearly that at least some members of the clan were feathered. It would be safe to say that later dromaeosaurs also possessed feathers, even if only at the early stages of their growth. *Microraptor* had long feathers on its forelimbs and hind limbs, effectively giving it four wings. It also had a phalanx of feathers lining the end of its tail. *Microraptor* was not a bird, though, and is considered a flightless feathered dinosaur that could probably glide. The evolution of feathers, which is described more fully in the next chapter, may have first come about to provide insulation for these animals. According to this hypothesis, the role of feathers in flight was a secondary application.

THE THEROPOD LEGACY

Non-avian theropods were among the first dinosaurs to evolve and certainly among the last to perish with the mass extinction at the end of the Cretaceous Period. Their legacy defines the size limits seen thus far for terrestrial predatory creatures but also demonstrates a remarkably diverse group of animals that evolved in many specialized directions. Theropods, along with sauropods, were among the most successful and long-lived lineages of dinosaurs because they outpaced changes to their environment by adapting increasingly specialized means for coping with food supplies, climate, and competition with other dinosaurs.

The greatest legacy of theropods may be that they are still among us today in the form of birds. No other kinds of dinosaurs can make that claim. The transition of dinosaurs to birds and their known links in the fossil record are explored in the next chapter.

SUMMARY

This chapter explored the last great families of carnivorous dinosaurs that flourished during the Early and Late Cretaceous Epochs.

1. Ceratosauria included many medium- to large-sized theropods of the Cretaceous Period, mostly in the Southern Hemisphere.
2. The Tetanurae ("stiff tails") represented the last great wave of predatory dinosaurs and also ultimately led to the emergence of birds. The Tetanurae is further divided into two major subgroups: the Spinosauroidea, consisting of the most primitive, least-derived, basal tetanurans; and the more derived Avetheropoda.
3. The largest predatory dinosaur was *Spinosaurus*, followed by several carcharodontosaurs, another spinosaur, and *Tyrannosaurus*.
4. The Avetheropoda had origins in the Middle Jurassic and consisted of several diverse subgroups representing the smallest known dinosaurs as well as some of the largest. It is also within the Avetheropoda ("bird theropods") that the first definitive link between dinosaurs and modern birds took place.
5. Carcharodontosaurs, including *Carcharodontosaurus* and *Giganotosaurus*, were among the most successful large predatory

dinosaurs of the Southern Hemisphere. There is evidence that at least one carcharodontosaur taxon, *Mapusaurus*, may have lived, hunted, and traveled in groups.

6. The Coelurosauria are divided into four main groups and then several subgroups. The tyrannosaurs included *T. rex* and its kin. The ornithomimosaurs were ostrichlike dinosaurs and possibly the fastest of all dinosaurs. The therizinosaurs were stocky bipeds with huge hand claws and a tendency toward an herbivorous diet. The maniraptorans included small to medium-sized theropods with close links to birds and birds themselves.

7. The discovery of the maniraptoran *Deinonychus*, a dromaeosaur from Montana, ignited modern debate over the lifestyle and lineage of dinosaurs and their relationship to birds.

4

THE ORIGIN OF BIRDS

Knowing that birds exist, not everyone is tempted to wonder how they evolved. Birds are so utterly familiar that we pay little attention as they walk near the curb in front of us, perch on a phone wire overhanging an intersection, and punctuate the ambient sound around us with their chittering, chirping, and occasional song. Ask anyone to explain what a bird is and that person will look at you with a suspicious grin. What is there to explain? Birds are birds. They have feathers; they fly; they poke into the mat of a newly mowed lawn to find insects to eat; they soar through the air with uncanny ease, going where they wish, seemingly with few inhibitions. "Free as a bird" is a familiar expression.

To explore the origin of birds, it is necessary to deconstruct every notion of what a bird is. We would not confuse a bird with any other animal today. A bird is nothing like a salamander, a dog, or a horse. Yet all of these are tetrapods—four-limbed vertebrates. In the Late Jurassic and Early Cretaceous Epochs, if you were to compare some small carnivorous dinosaurs to the first birds, the distinctions between the two would be difficult to make. Birds are, in fact, the surviving descendants of dinosaurs and have many anatomical parts that first evolved in their nonflying ancestors.

This chapter explores the evolution of birds from dinosaurs and provides a framework for understanding the origins of birds in the overall context of the world of the dinosaurs. A thorough exploration of the many kinds of modern families of birds is beyond the scope of this volume, which is focused primarily on non-avian dinosaurs. The diversification and radiation of modern birds expanded rapidly following the extinction of the dinosaurs. The evolutionary lines that make up modern birds are explored in another book in the *Prehistoric Earth* series, *The Rise of Mammals*, as one of the continuing stories of vertebrate evolution. The discussion of birds in this book, *Last of the Dinosaurs,* focuses on the most primitive, or basal, taxa that led to modern birds.

THE DINOSAUR-BIRD CONNECTION

Birds are dinosaurs just as snakes are reptiles and horses are mammals. The most prominent feature that distinguishes birds from other dinosaurs is their ability to fly. *Last of the Dinosaurs* uses the term *non-avian dinosaur* to refer to those dinosaurs that did not fly and are thus not considered true birds. The basal Avialae, or primitive birds, described in this chapter are defined as maniraptorans closer to birds than to *Deinonychus*, a dromaeosaurid. Some of these creatures flew and some did not, but all evolved from flying ancestors. All were part of an evolutionary trajectory leading to the anatomical and physiological traits now seen in birds.

Archaeopteryx is considered to be the first true bird, yet it retained many anatomical features that were not seen in later birds, such as teeth, a long and bony tail, and underdeveloped wings. *Archaeopteryx* also dates from the Late Jurassic, about 150 million years ago—about 25 million years before other known fossil specimens of early birds. That considerable gap in the fossil record has only recently begun to be filled with evidence of other stages in the evolution of small coelurosaurs into birds. Paleontologist Kevin Padian, one of the leading researchers on bird origins, explains that looking for fossil evidence of the earliest birds can best be done by looking for traits found in *Archaeopteryx* that are shared with later birds but which are not known in other vertebrates, and searching for such traits in non-avian theropods. If one were to seek evidence of other stages in the evolution of small coelurosaurs into birds, then one should look in Early and Middle Jurassic sediments, since the first known bird (*Archaeopteryx*) is Late Jurassic in age.

The extinct *Archaeopteryx* compared to the modern magpie

There is more than a superficial resemblance between dinosaurs and birds. Fossil evidence strongly supports an evolutionary transition in which birds were descended from dinosaurs. The discoveries described in these pages constitute a few of more than 120 anatomical features that were originally found in small meat-eating dinosaurs and inherited by birds, including:

- Lightweight skeletons with hollow bones.
- A furcula, or wishbone, found in many theropod groups, including the oviraptorosaurs *Ingenia* ("for Ingeni-Khobur"), *Oviraptor* ("egg thief"), and the dromaeosaur *Bambiraptor* ("Bambi thief").
- Teeth. Many early birds, including *Archaeopteryx*, had teeth like their dinosaur ancestors.
- Pygostyle-like structures at the tail tips of some birdlike dinosaurs, including oviraptorosaurs and therizinosaurs.
- Feathers or feather-like filaments ("protofeathers") in most coelurosaur groups, including compsognathids (*Sinosauropteryx*), tyrannosauroids (*Dilong*), therizinosaurs

(*Beipiaosaurus*), oviraptorosaurs (*Caudipteryx*, *Protarchaeopteryx*), troodontids (*Jinfengopteryx*), and dromaeosaurids (*Microraptor*, *Sinornithosaurus*, and probably *Velociraptor*).

- The ability to walk on two legs, supported by three weight-bearing toes.
- Dinosaurlike claws on birds such as *Archaeopteryx*, which had a dromaeosaurlike sickle-claw on the second toe of each foot.
- Birdlike shoulder and breast bones in some dinosaurs that allowed the arms to fold and move in the same fashion that primitive birds moved their wings. This trait was most pronounced in dromaeosaurs such as *Unenlagia* ("half-bird") from South America and *Bambiraptor* from Montana.
- Long arms in small theropods, comparable in length to the bones of bird wings. For instance, dromaeosaurs had relatively long arms compared with other theropod dinosaurs. Specifically, their forelimbs were nearly as long as, or possibly longer than, their hind limbs.
- The enlargement of the forebrain in non-avian theropod dinosaurs was a trend continued in birds, whose brain capacity is greater than that found in most dinosaurs.
- Egg laying and brooding behaviors. Dinosaurs and birds laid eggs, and there is evidence that some dinosaurs watched over their nests and young—a behavioral trait observed in modern birds.

Feather Origins

Feathers are a familiar trait associated with birds. Until recently, the presence of feather impressions in a fossil meant that a specimen was a bird. This assumption held true for *Archaeopteryx* in 1861 and remained unquestioned until the description of *Sinosauropteryx* in 1996. The skin of *Sinosauropteryx*, a non-avian dinosaur, was covered with protofeathers, but because that animal clearly could not fly, paleontologists had to entertain the possibility that the

Sinosauropteryx was a dromaeosaur with a fuzzy covering for insulation.

evolution of feathers and flight were not as intimately connected as had once been believed. Subsequent to the discovery of *Sinosauropteryx*, a host of discoveries of non-avian theropods, including those of *Sinornithosaurus* and *Caudipteryx*, showed irrefutable evidence that some small, flightless dinosaurs were equipped with feathers. By decoupling the presence of feathers from the ability to fly, it was possible to consider feathers as an inherited trait that birds acquired from non-avian dinosaur ancestors. It is now assumed that ancestral coelurosaurians had feathers before the evolution of birds.

The first feathers probably insulated small theropods from temperature extremes, allowing them to regulate their body temperature more effectively. Gradually, as the arms of some small coelurosaurs evolved into more winglike forelimbs, feathers that once were used solely for insulation acquired the secondary function of creating a feathered covering on the forelimb. These feathers served as an airfoil that enabled some theropods to glide and, later, to engage in powered flight.

Feathers are such unique, complex structures that they probably evolved only once. Birds and dinosaurs are the only creatures known to have had feathers. Unless other fossil evidence is found that might prove otherwise, the presence of feathers is one of the most compelling reasons to believe that birds evolved from small, feathered dinosaurs.

EVOLUTION OF FLIGHT IN BIRDS

Powered flight is not unique to birds. Insects, bats, and pterosaurs also evolved the ability to fly under their own power. Among animals with backbones, powered flight has evolved three separate times: first in the pterosaurs, then in birds, and finally in bats—each independent of one another. This is an example of **convergent evolution**, wherein different organisms evolve similar adaptations, often in response to analogous environmental stresses or opportunities.

There are three main anatomical requirements for flight that are shared by bats, pterosaurs, and birds:

- *Lightweight body.* Such a body has hollow bones and sometimes fewer bones in the back. Technically, bats do not have hollow bones, but the marrow cavity of their bones is proportionately larger than in other mammals, providing for a lighter-weight skeleton.
- *Airfoil to produce lift.* The wing is an airfoil. When combined with forward motion, it produces lift, the force that allows a body to become airborne.
- *Energy to initiate flight.* Most modern birds are strong enough to become airborne from a standing start.

Archaeopteryx may be the earliest known bird, but it is somewhat of an enigma when it comes to explaining the evolution of bird flight. Because there is very little fossil evidence of birdlike theropods that lived prior to *Archaeopteryx*, little is known about dinosaurian adaptations leading to the first bird. Two main hypotheses have been offered for the beginnings of bird flight. One hypothesis assumes that bird flight began as a *trees-down* phenomenon, probably with creatures that could glide from a tree to the ground before they evolved powered flight. The other hypothesis assumes a *ground-up* origin, in which small running dinosaurs gradually adapted their leaping and maneuvering into flapping flight.

The trees-down hypothesis is attractive because it assumes that gliding was possible in some coelurosaurs before they developed powered flight. One can easily imagine a feathered dinosaur or an early bird gliding down from a tree branch. It simply makes sense. As those coelurosaurs became more skilled at gliding, turning their bodies and feathered forelimbs to steer themselves and control their fall, they evolved the anatomical adaptations that resulted in powered flight many generations later. A requirement of the trees-down hypothesis is that it requires that some small dinosaurs were already climbing in trees. Evidence for theropods prior to *Archaeopteryx* that may have had claws well adapted for climbing trees is slim, but now includes two specimens from Inner Mongolia that may be from sediments of Middle Jurassic age. One of these, *Pedopenna* (possibly Middle Jurassic, Mongolia) might be the first record of a non-avian feathered dinosaur that lived before the time of *Archaeopteryx*. The other is a tiny non-avian **arboreal** dinosaur named *Epidendrosaurus*, which places some theropod dinosaurs in trees before the evolution of bird flight.

The ground-up hypothesis is more challenging to imagine, but it fits well with anatomical evidence observed in the skeletons of small predatory dinosaurs and early birds, with the exception of *Archaeoptyrx*, *Microraptor*, and *Epidendrosaurus*. According to this hypothesis, small feathered dinosaurs began to leap and improve their maneuverability while running along the ground. Running, dodging, and leaping would have been important strategies for catching food and also for escaping from other predators. A small dinosaur could become briefly airborne while doing this. The act of reaching forward with both hands to grasp prey might have led to the flapping motion seen later in powered flight. Over millions of years, the arms of some theropod dinosaurs gradually changed into wings as the development of their arms became more specialized. These creatures were evidently successful at surviving, and they passed along these traits to their offspring. *Archaeopteryx* seems to be a creature that evolved from the ground up because it still has the legs, feet, and hands of its ground-dwelling dinosaur ancestor.

There is growing evidence for the trees-down hypothesis. In addition to the recent discovery of the arboreal theropod *Epidendrosaurus*, the anatomy of the Early Cretaceous dromaeosaur *Microraptor* strongly suggests arboreal habits and locomotion by gliding. It may have had a tree-based lifestyle similar to flying squirrels today. These kinds of specimens strongly suggest that birds evolved from the "trees down," arboreal, gliding, non-avian theropods.

From Non-Avian to Avian Theropods

Explorers looking for the fossil origins of birds have been remarkably successful in the past 10 years in uncovering many spectacular clues to the origins of flight and of birds. Discoveries in the Southern and Northern Hemispheres of the Mesozoic world—from Argentina, Antarctica, and Madagascar to China, Central Asia, Spain, and the United States—have done much to fill the gap in our knowledge of bird evolution that once existed between the existence of *Archaeopteryx* in the Late Jurassic and the origin of anatomically modern birds by the end of the Cretaceous. What is now revealed is that bird evolution and the transformation of small theropod dinosaurs did not occur on a single evolutionary track, but on many parallel tracks that led to a diversity of creatures. One of these evolutionary pathways led to the birds we know today.

The plentiful fossil lake beds of Liaoning and neighboring provinces in northeastern China capture the significant diversity of life that existed there during the Early Cretaceous Epoch. Dating from a mere 25 million years after *Archaeopteryx*, these Chinese deposits hold unprecedented fossil evidence of a rich ecosystem and its inhabitants. Plant fossils abound, from seed-bearing cones to stems and fronds, and collectively document the presence of conifer and ginkgo trees, cycads, bennettitaleans, ferns, and the earliest known flowering plants. The arthropod kingdom is represented by myriad flying insects, spiders, crayfish, and other creatures. The vertebrates of Liaoning, however, deservedly steal the spotlight, for in these deposits are found a diverse group of small mammals, fluffy pterosaurs, birds, non-avian dinosaurs, aquatic reptiles, archaic and modern fishes, frogs, salamanders, turtles, and lizards. Living side by side were small non-avian feathered dinosaurs such as *Microraptor* and *Sinosauropteryx* and early birds of many kinds. There is a wealth of information relevant not only to determining the possible evolutionary relationships between clades of small, feathered dinosaurs and birds, but also to reconstructing a much more complex picture of bird evolution that defies simple, stage-by-stage linear explanation that would be tempting to maintain if no such wealth of fossils had been found.

The job of classifying and defining relationships between these many spectacular fossil animals relies heavily on **cladistic analysis** and the comparison of derived anatomical traits that were inherited from one species line to another. At least one lineage—that of birds—led to powered flight. Others, however, led simply to advanced, feathered, ground-dwelling non-avian dinosaurs. It is also possible that some lineages arose from flying ancestors and then summarily left flight behind, regaining a firm grip on the ground once again. There are many puzzles introduced by Liaoning fossils that will require many generations of paleontologists to understand with certainty.

The evolution of the flight mechanism of birds involved significant modification of the anatomy of the dinosaurian forelimb. In birds, the function of the hand and wrist are minimized: Hand and wrist are fused together, the hands lack prominent claws, and both hand and wrist function primarily as supports for the leading edge of the wing. The bird forelimb contains three fused digits—a relic of avian origins in the three-fingered non-avian theropods such as the dromaeosaur *Deinonychus*. Modern birds are toothless, with a horny bill; this is another trait that can be traced to traits first derived in dinosaurs. Birds have a large breastbone for the attachment of flight muscles;

collarbones that are fused into a wishbone (furcula); a short tail tipped with a pygostyle for the attachment of tail feathers; and a clawed foot with three weight-supporting toes that is nearly identical to the foot seen in predatory dinosaurs. The bones of birds are also hollow and lightweight.

The study of basal birds involves identifying various stages in the evolution of the above anatomical features of birds until the appearance of truly modern-looking birds. Each of the bird clades described below includes some, but not all, of these characteristics, thus making each clade primitive in terms of the evolution of the modern bird body plan.

Alternative Theories of Bird Origins

While the prevailing and best-received theory of bird origins is that the first birds evolved from non-avian maniraptoran dinosaurs, there are two competing ideas that need mentioning. The first idea, long held by a few paleontologists, including Alan Feduccia and Larry Martin (b. 1943), is that birds and maniraptorans evolved at the same time from a common archosaurian tetrapod ancestor yet to be discovered. That idea would most likely depend on a trees-down origin of powered flight in birds.

A more novel but well-conceived hypothesis is held by paleontologist and artist Gregory Paul, who holds that maniraptoran dinosaur taxa such as *Velociraptor* and *Deinonychus* were the nonflying descendants of birds that came before them. In arguing such an opposite sequence of events, Paul takes advantage of the anatomical similarities between dinosaurs and birds while also capitalizing on the fact that *Archaeopteryx* preceded the vast majority of maniraptorans in the fossil record. This hypothesis accepts the extraordinary similarities between theropod dinosaurs and birds as evidence of their close relationship.

Both of these alternative evolutionary sequences for the origin of birds are clouded by a scarcity of fossil evidence from the Middle and Late Jurassic Epochs that could better illuminate the true evolutionary relationship between the first birds and dinosaurs.

Until such fossil evidence is found, most paleontologists believe that the anatomical similarities shared by *Archaeopteryx* and Early Cretaceous maniraptorans and basal birds of the Early Cretaceous are adequate to prove that they are related in such a way that birds must have sprung from dinosaurs.

BASAL AVIALAE: FEATHERED DINOSAURS AND THE EARLIEST BIRDS

The clade of theropods known as **Avialae** is a natural group including all of the descendants of the common ancestor of *Archaeopteryx* and *Passer domesticus*, the modern house sparrow. The basal members of this clade, discussed below, consist of early avians that existed prior to the close of the Mesozoic Era. These creatures represent the transitional stages of evolution from *Archaeopteryx* to modern birds.

Anatomical traits that unite these avian theropods include long forelimbs; a pointed premaxilla; small teeth that were not serrated; modifications of the shoulder, sternum, and pelvis to accommodate flight-related locomotion; and changes to the hands and feet, among others. The presence of feathers is almost certainly a shared trait but cannot be known from all fossils because of preservational biases.

The basal Avialae are divided into seven main subgroups: the Archaeopterygidae, Confuciusornithidae, Enantiornithes, Ornithurae, Hesperornthes, Ichthyornithiformes, and Neornithes. Each of these separate groups features primitive traits of the next and are viewed from an evolutionary standpoint as nested groups; you might picture the evolutionary relationships of the basal Avialae as being like that of Russian nesting dolls. The accompanying figure illustrates the relationships of basal birds and non-avian maniraptoran dinosaurs.

Archaeopterygidae

The Archaeopterygidae is a group including only the first known bird, *Archaeopteryx*, from the Late Jurassic of Germany. *Archaeopteryx* is represented by several excellent, two-dimensional

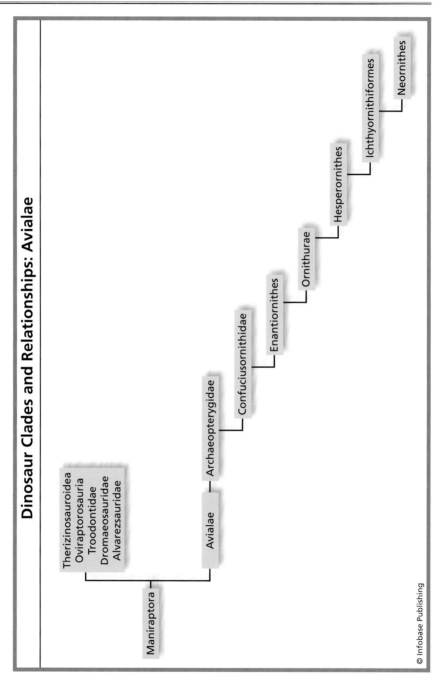

Dinosaur Clades and Relationships: Avialae

Maniraptora

Therizinosauroidea
Oviraptorosauria
Troodontidae
Dromaeosauridae
Alvarezsauridae

Avialae

Archaeopterygidae

Confuciusornithidae

Enantiornithes

Ornithurae

Hesperornithes

Ichthyornithiformes

Neornithes

© Infobase Publishing

(flattened) fossil skeletons, many of which include skulls and/or feather impressions. *Archaeopteryx* has been called the most valuable of all fossils because of its importance in understanding the evolution of species. At the time of its discovery in the early 1860s, Charles Darwin had only recently proposed his theory of evolution by natural selection. Darwin himself relied primarily on observations of living species to explain his case for evolution. Evolution is a process that typically requires millions of years, however, and his opponents argued, even then, that anatomical transitions from one species to another were difficult to ascertain from the observation of living species alone. *Archaeopteryx* provided another kind of evidence entirely, blending the features of reptiles with those of birds from the very annals of time, demonstrating in a single fossil taxon that one species could likely evolve into another and that the process of avian evolution had been taking place for tens of millions of years.

Diagnostic traits that were found in these first recognized birds included small, sharp teeth in upper and lower jaws, five fused sacral vertebrae, and lack of a bony breastbone that were specific to *Archaeopteryx*. These same creatures had other obviously dinosaurian features such as a long, bony tail and sharply clawed fingers and toes, but those traits were less unique to the Archaeopterygidae than the specific nature of their teeth, jaws, and limb girdles.

Confuciusornithidae

The Confuciusornithidae is another small clade of primitive birds, but it is represented by hundreds of complete specimens of its best-known taxon, *Confuciusornis* (Early Cretaceous, China). All three known taxa of confuciusornithids were discovered in the exquisite fossil deposits of Liaoning and neighboring provinces in northeastern China.

These basal birds were closer to modern birds than was *Archaeopteryx* and had already shed most of the traits of non-avian dinosaurs—teeth and a long tail—that had been retained by *Archaeopteryx*. *Confuciusornis* was about the size of a crow. It had a pygostyle, or shortened tail tip composed of coalesced vertebrae, for the attachment of tail feathers, but it still retained long, curved claws on its wings—a trait considered a primitive or basal bird trait. The Confuciousornithidae share some similarities with the dromaeosaur

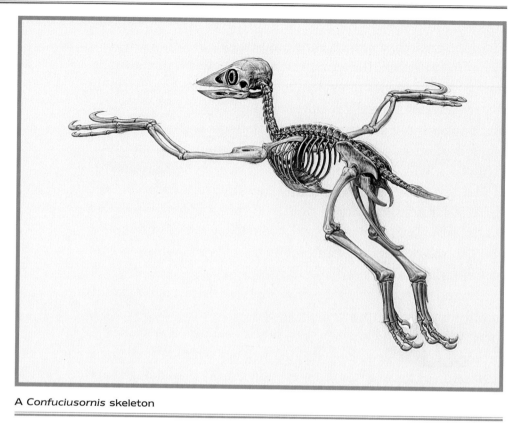

A *Confuciusornis* skeleton

Microraptor; this suggests a close relationship with that line of non-avian coelurosaurian dinosaur.

A primitive feature that *Confuciusornis* shared with *Archaeopteryx* was found in the wings. The shoulder bones of *Confuciusornis* were oriented in such a way as to have prevented the kind of upstroke required for the type of flapping flight seen in modern birds. Confuciusornithids most certainly were adequate fliers, but they may have managed powered flight with a shallow, jolting thrust of the wings that would seem quite peculiar when compared with modern birds.

At least one specimen of *Confuciusornis* has been found with evidence of a last meal in its remains. In 2006, Swedish paleontologist J. Dalsätt and colleagues reported finding a specimen with fish remains in its throat. This suggests that confuciusornithids were either fish eaters or omnivorous.

Enantiornithes

The Enantiornithes ("opposite birds") clade was established in 1981, based on some scattered postcranial elements discovered in Argentina by paleontologist José Bonaparte and scientifically described by C.A. Walker. Walker described the namesake of the clade, *Enantiornis* (Late Cretaceous, Argentina), noting that the fusion of bones in its feet and ankles differed from other birds. In modern birds, the foot bones, or metatarsals, are fused together from the middle bone to the outward bones. The metatarsals of *Enantiornis* were fused from the direction of the ankle toward the toes—the opposite of other birds and hence the bird's name. Since the discovery of *Enantiornis*, a host of other similar birds have been discovered.

The Enantiornithes were the most diverse and geographically widespread of all Cretaceous birds. Anatomically, these birds were not as basal as *Archaeopteryx* but not as derived as modern birds. They shared such traits as a relatively long tail capped by a short, fused pygostyle; a bony but weakly developed breastbone; a Y-shaped wishbone; similar limb elements; and toothed jaws—although some later species were toothless.

Early discoveries of Enantiornithes consisted primarily of fragmentary specimens, and it was difficult to paint a complete picture of the clade with certainty. *Neuquenornis* (Late Cretaceous, Argentina) was described by paleontologists Luis Chiappe and Jorge Calvo in 1994 and was based upon a partial skeleton that included most of the traits of this group in one specimen.

Enantiornis was a taxon of large birds with a wingspan of about 4 feet (1.2 m), but most other members of the clade were about the size of a sparrow or thrush. These birds also adapted to many lifestyles and habitats, with different taxa finding home in the trees, on the ground, and perhaps in the water as waders or swimmers. Enantiornithes are currently known from more than 25 taxa hailing from every continent but Antarctica. They apparently all became extinct at the end of the Cretaceous Period, alongside the last non-avian dinosaurs.

Sinornis (Early Cretaceous, China), the "Chinese bird," was described by Paul Sereno and Chenggang Rao in 1992 and based primarily on a nearly complete skeleton. Living about 25 million years after *Archaeopteryx*, its shortened body, pygostyle, and folding wings made it closer to the body plan of a modern bird, but it still had teeth, clawed fingers, and a small breast bone.

Eoalulavis (Early Cretaceous, Spain), the "dawn alula bird," had many anatomical improvements for flight over *Archaeopteryx* and other basal birds. Most notably, it had the oldest known alula, a set of feathers on the front edge of the bird's wing that helped sustain lift as the bird flew at slow speeds.

Other noteworthy Enantiornithes for which there is convincing fossil evidence are *Aberratiodontus* (Early Cretaceous, China); *Alexornis* (Late Cretaceous, Mexico); *Bolouchia* (Early Cretaceous, China); *Concornis* (Early Cretaceous, Spain); *Dapingfangornis* (Early Cretaceous, China); *Elsornis* (Late Cretaceous, Mongolia); *Eocathayornis* (Early Cretaceous, China); *Eoenantiornis* (Early Cretaceous, China); *Gobipteryx* (Late Cretaceous, Mongolia); *Halimornis* (Late Cretaceous, Alabama); *Iberomesornis* (Early Cretaceous, Spain); *Longipteryx* (Early Cretaceous, China); *Longirostravis* (Early Cretaceous, China); *Otogornis* (Early Cretaceous, China); *Protopteryx* (Early Cretaceous, China); and *Vescornis* (Early Cretaceous, China).

Ornithuromorpha

The clade Ornithuromorpha includes modern, extant birds and all extinct basal birds whose traits were closer to those of modern birds than to Enantiornithes. In addition to including the Neornithes, or "new birds," ornithuromorphs encompassed several basal taxa. In contrast to more primitive birds and non-avian theropods, the ornithuromorphs had a well-developed pygostyle and short, bony tails, and a suite of anatomical traits of the shoulder and breast bones, furcula, wrist, hands, and pelvis that improved the flying ability of these early birds.

Basal members of the Ornithuromorpha, including *Chaoyangia*, *Yanornis*, *Yixianornis*, *Hongshanornis*, *Archaeorhynchus*, and *Gansus* from Early Cretaceous deposits in China, represent various transitional phases between primitive, enantiornitheanlike birds and modern birds. *Gansus* was perhaps the most advanced of these birds. Until recently, this bird was known only from a partial hind limb described in 1984. A series of joint Chinese-American expeditions to Gansu Province from 2004 to 2007 uncovered dozens of new specimens that now provide a much more complete picture of this animal. It was a semi-aquatic, loonlike bird with webbed feet.

Hesperornithes

The Hesperornithes were a highly specialized subgroup of aquatic ornithuromorphs. Also loonlike but probably all flightless, these large birds measured up to 3.3 feet (1 m) long and were divers. There are about nine valid taxa of Hesperornithes and they are definitely known only from fossil localities in the Northern Hemisphere.

The best-known hesperornithean is *Hesperornis* (Late Cretaceous, western North America), for which several skulls and partial skeletons have been found. When it was first described by legendary Yale paleontologist O.C. Marsh in 1872, this bird created quite a sensation, for, like *Archaeopteryx*, it retained teeth from its dinosaurian ancestors. In most other respects, however, it was anatomically close to modern birds. In addition to very reduced wings and a long beak and legs, *Hesperornis* had a longer fourth toe than most birds, and it has been suggested that, like a penguin, this bird probably waddled when it walked on land.

Ichthyornithiformes

The Ichthyornithiformes were another group of seabirds from the Late Cretaceous. There is currently only one definitively recognized taxon, *Ichthyornis* (Late Cretaceous, American Midwest), so named "fish bird" because of the resemblance of its vertebrae to those of fish. Although the body of this bird was mostly modern, its large and long skull retained small teeth in its jaws—a feature not found in modern birds.

THE RISE OF BIRDS

Until recently, the only known feathered creatures—extant or extinct—were birds. Having feathers was also synonymous with having wings, a truism that held even for most flightless birds such as the penguin. *Archaeopteryx*, despite its resemblance to dinosaurs, was immediately recognized as a bird because it had wings and feathers.

Recent fossil discoveries, particularly in China, have proven those assumptions incorrect. There are now excellent fossil examples of more than a dozen coelurosaurian theropod dinosaurs that had feathers or featherlike structures but could not fly. These non-avian theropods, mostly small-bodied, probably originally developed feathers as a way to keep warm.

The discovery of non-avian feathered dinosaurs reinforces one of the fundamental practices of scientific investigation: the detection and correction of error. Paleontologists know this only too well, for how many times have claims been made based only on partial fossil evidence to be corrected later by the discovery of more informative specimens? It happens all of the time in the study of past life.

SUMMARY

This chapter explored the evolution of birds from dinosaurs and provided a framework for understanding their origins in the overall context of the world of the dinosaurs.

1. Birds are the surviving descendants of dinosaurs and retain many anatomical traits that first evolved in their non-flying ancestors.

2. *Archaeopteryx*, the first true bird, retained many archaic anatomical features—such as teeth, a long and bony tail, a cartilaginous breastbone, and clawed, underdeveloped wings—that are not seen in modern birds.

3. Traits shared by birds include lightweight skeletons with hollow bones; a furcula (or wishbone); a short, bony tail tipped with a pygostyle; feathers; wings; bipedal posture; and four clawed toes.

4. The first birds evolved from non-avian maniraptoran dinosaurs.

5. Feathers first appeared on non-avian theropods, probably as a way to insulate the body.

6. Two main hypotheses of the evolution of flight include the "trees-down" and "ground-up" concepts. The "trees-down" concept is most widely accepted by paleontologists.

7. The basal Avialae is divided into four principal groups, from least to most like modern birds; Archaeopterygidae, Confuciusornithidae, Enantiornithes, and Ornithuromorpha, the latter including three main subgroups: Hesperornithes, Ichthyornithiformes, and Neornithes.

SECTION THREE:
ORNITHISCIAN
DINOSAURS OF THE
CRETACEOUS PERIOD

5

Iguanodontids and Hadrosaurs

Ornithischian dinosaurs made up one of the two major clades of dinosaurs. The ornithischians were united, among other features, by a generalized design of the pelvis known as a "bird," or ornithischian, hip. Note that the ornithischian "bird" hip has only a superficial resemblance to actual birds (saurischians) discussed in the previous chapter; the two kinds of dinosaur hips are thought to have arisen independently.

Including a variety of bipedal and quadrupedal herbivores, ornithischians were highly successful and specialized plant eaters, many of which grew to large size and lived in herds. Ornithischians had evolutionary roots in the Late Triassic but were overshadowed early on by the more dominant saurischians, including theropods, prosauropods, and sauropods. The most visible ornithischians of the Jurassic Period were armored, plated, and basal ornithopod dinosaurs, but even their success was trumped by the "bird-hipped" herbivores of the Cretaceous. It was during the last great surge of dinosaur evolution that several new and sophisticated plant-eating clades of ornithischian dinosaurs arose and radiated across the globe. This was the time of the iguanodontids, the hadrosaurs, and the horned and bone-headed dinosaurs, as well as a few remaining taxa of plated, armored, and basal ornithopodan ornithischians.

Ornithischians represented the crowning achievement of sophisticated plant-eating jaw design in dinosaurs. The horned dinosaurs and hadrosaurids in particular had dental batteries so well suited for chewing plants that they rival those seen in later mammals. This burst of innovation in the chewing mechanisms of later dinosaurs occurred at the same time as the rise of the angiosperms—the flowering plants. Because angiosperms were, on average, more nutritious than gymnosperms and other more ancient plants, most researchers conclude that the Late Cretaceous burst of ornithischian dinosaur evolution was literally fueled by the flowering plants, a new and better source of nutrition for dinosaurs. This section of *Last of the Dinosaurs* explores the major groups of Cretaceous ornithischian dinosaurs, beginning in this chapter with the iguanodontids and hadrosaurids. This chapter is followed by one that describes the horned and bone-headed dinosaurs and another that examines the last of the armored and plated dinosaurs.

The clade **Ornithischia** is defined by several anatomical traits shared by all of its members. The clade is considered a natural group of dinosaurs sharing a common ancestor. All ornithischians were herbivorous; some were bipedal and others quadrupedal. Ornithischia is further divided into two large subgroups: the Thyreophora, consisting of the armored and plated dinosaurs, and the Cerapoda, consisting of the additional subgroups Ornithopoda (iguanodontids, hadrosaurs, and others) and Marginocephalia (Ceratopsia or horned dinosaurs and Pachycephalosauria, the bone-headed dinosaurs). The ornithischians described in this chapter fall within the Ornithopoda.

The subgroup Ornithopoda ("bird-footed") includes bipedal, herbivorous ornithischian dinosaurs that were not armored. They include *Iguanodon* ("iguana tooth"), one of the first dinosaurs ever described, and the hadrosaur, or "duck-billed" dinosaurs, so named because their spoonlike mouth resembled that a duck. Ornithopods filled a place in nature that is today occupied by cattle, deer, horses, antelopes, and other medium-sized hoofed herbivores; ornithopods provided a steady supply of food for predators. There is evidence that many ornithopods traveled in great herds, nested in large colonies to lay their eggs, and took care of their young until their offspring were large enough to fend for themselves. Unlike some other plant-eating dinosaurs that had armor horns, ornithopods had few special defenses other than speed and, in some cases, size. Many Cretaceous ornithopods were in the size range of 25 to 30 feet (7.5 to 9 m) long. There also were some enormous taxa such as *Shantungosaurus* (Late Cretaceous, China) and *Lambeosaurus* (Late Cretaceous, Alberta and Mexico) that could reach lengths of 50 feet (15 m).

There are a number of ornithopods considered too primitive to be members of the Iguanodontia. *Heterodontosaurus* (Early Jurassic, South Africa) was one of the earliest—a small bipedal plant-eater with closely packed cheek teeth in its jaws, a sign of things to come. Several lines of primitive ornithopods thrived all the way to the end of the Cretaceous Period, finding niches in the shadows of their larger cousins.

Hypsilophodon (Early Cretaceous, England and Spain) is one of the better-known examples and is somewhat typical of basal ornithopods. Measuring between 4 and 7 feet (1.2 to 2.1 m) long, *Hypsilophodon* ("Hypsilophus tooth") had more derived cheek teeth than did *Heterodontosaurus*, with an arrangement of tightly packed, chisel-shaped teeth that overlapped when the jaw was closed to form a long cutting surface. The way in which the teeth rubbed together may have made them self-sharpening. This jaw adaptation allowed *Hypsilophodon* to shred its food and chew it to a pulp before swallowing. These animals may have had a pouchlike cheek that could hold excess food until it could be chewed. A primitive trait of *Hypsilophodon* was a set of small, plucking teeth in its premaxilla, the front portion of the upper jaw.

Other basal ornithopods for which relatively good fossil specimens exist are *Bugenasaura* (Late Cretaceous, western North America); *Gasparinisaura* (Late Cretaceous, Argentina); *Jeholosaurus* (Early Cretaeous, China); *Orodromeus* (Late Cretaceous, Alberta and Montana); *Oryctodromeus* (Late Cretaceous, Montana); *Parksosaurus* (Late Cretaceous, Alberta); *Thescelosaurus* (Late Cretaceous, western North America); *Yandusaurus* (Middle Jurassic, China); and *Zephyrosaurus* (Early Cretaceous, Montana).

THE IGUANODONTIA

The significance of the iguanodonts to the history of dinosaur science is a matter of record. In the year 1822—19 years before the term *dinosaur* became a part of scientific literature—a physician and amateur geologist named Gideon Mantell (1790–1852) was visiting a patient near Lewes, in the English countryside. Accompanying him was his wife, Mary Ann. As the story goes, while the doctor tended to his patient, Mary Ann took a stroll along a country road, where she noticed a jumbled pile of fossils and rocks that had been dug up because of a road repair. Recognizing that some of the fossils resembled teeth, she brought them to the attention of her husband.

Both Mantells were quite familiar with fossil finds from the area, particularly of invertebrates. Mary Ann often provided scientific illustrations for papers and books that Gideon wrote from time to time describing such specimens. Greatly excited by his wife's discovery, Mantell continued the search for more pieces of the fossil creature and wrote a memoir describing it in the same year. Most importantly, Mantell and his wife recognized that the remains were from a large animal with reptilian affinities, and his paper became the first to correctly describe such fossils as being those of a large, unique reptilian creature that had become extinct.

The Mantells continued their search for such fossils, and after having procured some additional evidence for their ancient saurian, Gideon wrote another paper in 1825 and gave the creature the name *Iguanodon* ("iguana tooth"). The first dinosaur ever described was an ornithopod.

Iguanodon has since become one of the best-known ornithopods, partly because of the remarkable discovery in the 1880s of more than 26 nearly complete and associated skulls and skeletons in a mine in Belgium. Currently, there are more than two dozen recognized taxa of nonhadrosaurid iguanodonts, including basal forms, iguanodontids such as *Iguanodon* itself, and animals on the line to hadrosaurids.

Nonhadrosaurid iguanodonts are noted for having a toothless premaxilla with a deeply rounded snout and large, anterior nasal opening. They ranged in size from small, basal members measuring 6.6 to 10 feet (2 to 3 m) long to the largest members that were up to 37 feet (11 m) long. The fossil record of iguanodonts is well documented and shows remarkable stages of transformation in the size, posture, and dental adaptations of the clade.

Some of the primitive iguanodonts, such as *Dryosaurus* (Late Jurassic, western North America and Tanzania); *Tenontosaurus* (Early Cretaceous, western North America); and *Camptosaurus* (Late Jurassic, western North America and England) illustrate adaptive stages leading to the larger iguanodontids and hadrosaurs. Many of these early members had long arms and were partly quadrupedal. The feet of *Tenontosaurus* and *Camptosaurus* were four-toed, while those of *Dryosaurus* had three weight-bearing toes, as was the case with more derived iguanodonts. The tails of iguanodonts also modified over time into a deep, stiff counter-balance that probably aided the animals in walking bipedally.

The evolution of iguanodonts from basal forms into taxa such as *Iguanodon* also involved increasingly robust adaptations to their plant-grinding jaws. The front of the jaws had become a tough, toothless beak for snipping off stems and twigs. The skull was long and narrow with an impressive row of ridged grinding teeth in each cheek. The upper and lower jaws each had about fifty closely packed, chisel-shaped teeth that formed a long grinding surface. Most animals that can grind food with their teeth, including cows and people, can move the lower jaw up and down as well as side to side. *Iguanodon* could not do this. Its lower jaw could only move up and down. Instead, it evolved a way to spread the upper jaw sideways to rub the inner surface of its upper teeth against the outer surface of the lower teeth. This movement was propelled by powerful jaw muscles, allowing *Iguanodon* to thoroughly grind the fibrous plants that it ate.

Large iguanodonts such as *Iguanodon* were probably slow-moving, making them subject to attack by predatory dinosaurs. Like many other ornithopods, iguanodonts probably survived by

Iguanodon could protect itself by using its spike thumbs to stab predators; this early example of a lively depiction of Iguanodon was rendered in the 1960s and is based on the best-known facts at that time.

breeding in large numbers and living in herds. When faced with defending itself, *Iguanodon* had stout spikes for thumbs that could have been used to stab its attackers.

Iguanodon and its close relatives are mostly known from the Northern Hemisphere and were quite populous in what is now Europe and Asia. A few such taxa have been found south of the Equator, including *Lurdusaurus* (Early Cretaceous, Niger) and *Ouranosaurus* (Early Cretaceous, Niger). *Ouranosaurus* is noted for having extraordinarily long spines on its back that may have formed a sail. If such a sail was indeed present, its function is not entirely understood, but it has been interpreted variously as a visual signaling mechanism (e.g., for recognizing individuals or gender differences) or for regulation of body temperature. The presence of another tall-spined but unrelated dinosaur—*Spinosaurus*, a predator best known from Egypt and Morocco—from the same tropical region lends some credence to the need for these large animals to have adapted an anatomical means for effectively venting heat, or even absorbing it from the Sun during the cooler hours of the day.

THE HADROSAURIDAE

The advanced iguanodontian ornithopods known as the Hadrosauridae ("bulky lizards") include some of the best-understood dinosaur taxa because of the abundance of their specimens and often because of excellent preservation. Hadrosaurs evolved some of the most effective methods for eating plants ever seen. These dinosaurs had more teeth than any other known land animals. There are more than 35 scientifically accepted taxa of hadrosaurs.

Hadrosaurs have also played an important role in the understanding of dinosaur anatomy and behavior. The first irrefutable evidence that some dinosaurs walked on two legs was the result of Joseph Leidy's description in 1868 of *Hadrosaurus* (Late Cretaceous, New Jersey), the first dinosaur discovered with forelimbs that were clearly not adapted for walking. The elaborate, often hollow crests observed in hadrosaurs have implications for vocalization and behavior, and also provide evidence of **sexual dimorphism** in dinosaurs. The discovery of eggs, nests, and hatchlings of *Maiasaura* (Late Cretaceous, Montana) and other hadrosaurs has been interpreted as evidence for parental care in the early stages of these dinosaurs' lives. The existence of excellent growth series of several hadrosaur species has revealed much about the metabolism and growth rate of dinosaurs. Some unique, naturally "mummified" specimens of hadrosaurs contain large patches of skin impressions, revealing much about the pattern and size of dinosaur scales. Some of these duckbill "mummies" may even preserve remnants of muscles, internal organs, and stomach contents.

The hadrosaurs were the last significant group of ornithopods to evolve. North American hadrosaurs such as *Edmontosaurus* lived in a world occupied by other familiar dinosaurs, including *Ankylosaurus*, *Triceratops*, and *Tyrannosaurus,* and were among the last kinds of dinosaurs to exist before the mass-extinction event at the end of the Cretaceous Period.

The skulls and jaws of hadrosaurs are their most diagnostic features, or traits. Without a skull, it is sometimes difficult to tell one hadrosaur taxon from another because of the similarities in their postcranial skeletons. Hadrosaurs are classified into two main groups based principally on the anatomy of the skull: Hadrosaurinae and Lambeosaurinae.

The hadrosaurines had solid head crests or no head crest at all. Representative hadrosaurines included some giants of the duck-billed dinosaurs, such as *Edmontosaurus* (Late Cretaceous, western North America) and *Shantungosaurus*. Hadrosaurine skulls were boxlike with a large nasal opening in the front. A few, such as *Saurolophus* (Late Cretaceous, Alberta and Mongolia) had a solid bony crest on the top of the head.

The lambeosaurines had long, narrow skulls with a hollow crest on top of the head. The morphology of their crests differed from one taxon to another, but all of the crests functioned as extensions of the nasal passages and may have been involved in display, sound production, or olfaction. Familiar lambeosaurines include *Parasaurolophus, Corythosaurus,* and *Lambeosaurus,* all from the Late Cretaceous of western North America. A host of

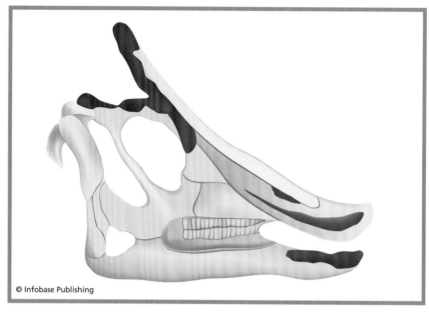

© Infobase Publishing

Saurolophus skull with a bony crest at the top of its head

new, remarkable lambeosaurines have recently come to light from the latest Cretaceous of far eastern Russia and China, such as *Charonosaurus*, *Olorotitan*, and *Sahaliyania*.

The jaws of hadrosaurs contained advanced dental batteries for grinding plants. Like the iguanodontids, duckbills could move their upper jaws sideways to rub their upper teeth across the full surface of the lower teeth. Rather than having the chisel-like teeth found in other ornithopods, hadrosaurs developed tightly packed rows of interlocking teeth. The teeth were layered so that new teeth continuously replaced old teeth. A duck-billed jaw had between 550 and 1,400 such teeth, most of which lay below the grinding surface and became active as the tooth layer at the surface was worn away. Hadrosaur teeth were so tightly packed that they formed a long, smooth pavement for chewing; this surface functioned as a magnified version of a metal file. These teeth were strong enough to pulverize the toughest kinds of plants with ease yet were adaptable to the kinds of softer, flowering plants that were beginning to populate their world.

Head variation among hadrosaurs

Other features shared by hadrosaurs include a functionally bipedal posture and shorter forelimbs than hind limbs; three weight-supporting toes on their hind feet; long, stiffened tails held off of the ground; a relatively long and slender neck; and four-fingered hands, some fingers of which were joined together by a covering of skin, making a kind of mittenlike structure. Although

(continues on page 128)

THINK ABOUT IT

The Form and Function of Hadrosaur Crests

The crested lambeosaurine hadrosaurs displayed an enormous variety of helmets, hatchets, and hood ornaments on their skulls. As a functional piece of anatomy, the crest was part of the nose. Fossil hadrosaurs, for which a cross-section of the skull can be observed, show that the nostrils were connected to the throat by a hollow set of cavities and tubes through which the dinosaur breathed. Most other kinds of dinosaurs did not have such crests, however, so we may assume that hollow crests had a special function other than breathing. What other purpose did such a crest have?

Crests came in a number of shapes. The crest of *Corythosaurus* ("helmet lizard") was rounded like a dinner plate standing on end, its base being thick to accomodate air passages. The crest associated with *Lambeosaurus* resembled a hatchet. The tube-like crest of *Parasaurolophus* was so long that it extended behind the head and over the shoulder. And the crest of the recently discovered *Olorotitan* looked something like a battle ax.

Many ideas have been suggested over the years for the purpose of these head crests. One early hypothesis regarding the crest of *Parasaurolophus* was that it may have been used like a snorkel. Because there is no evidence that these crests had a "breathing hole" at the end, however, this idea is no longer accepted.

Moreover, these crests may have had more than one function. It is likely that such a crest improved the dinosaur's sense of smell. This would have been important to relatively defenseless creatures such as hadrosaurs, allowing them to detect the scent of a predator from a safe distance.

The crest probably helped members of the same species recognize one another, a vital need for recognizing and choosing a mate. In 1975, paleontologist Peter Dodson conducted a groundbreaking study of lambeosaurine head crests and determined that they first became prominent when the animals reached the age of sexual maturity. Furthermore, females probably had smaller and differently-shaped crests than males. Although Dodson's conclusions have been universally accepted for many years, a recent study suggests that some of the specimens of "males" and "females" that he used for comparison came from different stratigraphic layers, meaning that they may not have actually lived at the same time. Nonetheless, crest shape could have helped to tell the boys from the girls, making the job of finding a mate easier. The shape and color of the crest may have made certain males or females more attractive than others. It would have also indicated the relative age and sexual maturity of an individual. In the world of animal matchmaking, those kinds of visual clues were important for bringing together healthy mates.

Another function of the crest might have been to create and project sounds, an idea that was thoroughly explored by paleontologist David Weishampel in 1981. Lambeosaurines could blow air through the tubes and hollow chambers of the crest to create bellowing sounds possibly similar to those made by an antique car horn or elephant. The sounds may have been important to hadrosaur communication. They could have used their voices to warn of approaching danger, call for help, or to express themselves for other reasons.

Knowledge of the sound-making ability of lambeosaurines was advanced in 1999 by paleontologists Thomas Williamson and Robert Sullivan, based on a new and remarkably complete skull of *Parasaurolophus*. Using computed tomography and modeling to examine and reconstruct the interior of the skull, the scientists not only produced a map of the interior air passages of the crest but also electronically synthesized the kinds of sounds that could be made using such a crest. Whereas previous knowledge of the *Parasaurolophus* crest concluded that its inner chambers simply consisted of two parallel, hollow tubes, Williamson and Sullivan revealed that the two tubes from the nostrils actually branched into as many as six tubes that were additionally interconnected to supplemental

(continues)

(continued)

air chambers in other parts of the crest. In addition to producing a wide variety of sounds, the paleontologists concluded that the crest may have served a thermoregulatory function. The inside of the *Parasaurolophus* crest was lined with blood vessels. Heat could have been collected by the crest if the head was turned toward the Sun or released if the head was held in the shadows. The air passages in the crest would have allowed the dinosaur to transfer heat more efficiently by passing hot and cold air through the head.

(continued from page 125)

technically bidpedal, the hadrosaur body plan also accommodated a part-time quadrupedal stance if needed, and these dinosaurs often are pictured using both styles of walking.

Fossil Skin Impressions

An abundance of fossilized skin impressions have been associated with specimens of hadrosaurs. These trace fossils left the pattern of the animal's skin in the mud where a given dinosaur died. All of the evidence uncovered so far regarding the skin of unfeathered dinosaurs shows that they had nonoverlapping scales similar to those of the modern monitor lizard. These scales varied in size across different parts of the body. The scales were generally smaller, for flexibility, around the head and very movable areas such as the neck and joints. Scales were larger along broad parts of the body and tail. The shapes of the individual scales were generally round or oval, and the scales were fitted together like a flattened mosaic of beads. In many dinosaur species for which skin is known, the scales were occasionally interrupted by much larger tubercles.

Additional information about the skin of ornithopods comes from several extremely rare, naturally "mummified" hadrosaur fossils. In such cases, the body of the dinosaur probably dried in the hot sun before being buried, undisturbed by scavengers. The skin of the creature was stretched tight over its bones as it dried. Even though the skin itself eventually disintegrated, the process of fossilization preserved the skin pattern across much of the specimen. One such dinosaur mummy on display at the American Museum of Natural History is that of a specimen of *Edmontosaurus* lying on its side with its right forelimb raised over its head. Other hadrosaur mummies have been discovered in recent years, such as the *Brachylophosaurus* "Leonardo," and "Dakota," another *Edmontosaurus*.

ORNITHOPOD LIFESTYLES

An abundance of fossil specimens of iguanodontids and hadrosaurs has led to important studies involving the nature of dinosaurs as living creatures. While the bones themselves can rarely tell the whole story of a living, breathing animal, a collection of evidence that combines skeletal remains with information about the habitat, social structure, neighbors, and circumstances of a dinosaur's death can lead to insight regarding that dinosaur's behavior and physiology.

Some of the most exciting research being done about dinosaur behavior and physiology comes from the study of ornithopods. Three such areas of interest include dinosaur growth rates, nesting and parental care, and sexual dimorphism in hadrosaurs.

Ornithopod Growth

Newly hatched dinosaurs were small, yet they sometimes grew to enormous sizes that were anywhere from 10 times to thousands of times their original weight. To understand how fast a given dinosaur grew, paleontologists rely on a growth series, a set of fossil skeletons of that taxon that represents several life stages. Such examples are available in abundance for some hadrosaurs, especially *Maiasaura* ("good mother lizard"). The bones can then be sliced open and examined under a microscope for biological clues to growth.

Bones grow thicker and longer as an animal matures. The microscopic patterns laid down by bones as they grow provide clues to the rate of growth. Bones, however, do not typically grow in a uniform manner throughout the life of a vertebrate. At one extreme, bones show a smooth, continuous pattern that indicates that the animal was growing continuously and rapidly without pause. At the other extreme, some bone tissue forms visible rings called *lines of arrested growth*. These growth rings are much like the seasonal rings in cross sections of tree trunks and represent times of slower growth, when the bone tissue is much denser. Lines of arrested growth can indicate the passage of a periodic, possibly annual period during which growth slows down, such as a change from a warm season to a cool season, a time during which an animal is less active for an extended period.

Some dinosaurs have both kinds of bone tissue. This means that such dinosaurs grew at different rates at different times in their lives. They appear to have grown rapidly until they reached adult size and then slowed down but continued to grow throughout the rest of their lives.

The bones of *Maiasaura* indicate that this duckbill required only about seven years to reach its maximum length of 30 feet (9 meters). During its first few years of growth, it did not deposit growth rings, suggesting that it grew continuously without seasonal interruptions. *Maiasaura* reached adult size about twice as fast as crocodiles and humans. Growing up fast was important for these dinosaurs because they were defenseless against predators until they were large enough to use their bulk for protection.

The growth rates of hadrosaurs should be not assumed for other clades of dinosaurs. A study in 2006 by paleontologist Andy Lee focused on the growth rates of horned dinosaurs and found that *Psittacosaurus* reached maturity in 8 to 13 years, *Protoceratops* in about seven years, and about six years in the large *Centrosaurus*. Within the ornithopods, the basal iguanodontian *Dryosaurus*, the basal ornithopod *Orodromeus*, and the hadrosaur *Hypacrosaurus* (Late Cretaceous, Alberta) all showed similarly moderate to rapid growth at a young age and an absence of growth rings until these dinosaurs reached maturity.

Sexual Dimorphism

Sexual dimorphism occurs when male and female individuals of a single species exhibit different anatomical traits. Such traits can be determined reliably in dinosaurs only when an abundance of specimens from the same species can be compared. Such traits helped dinosaurs distinguish male individuals of their species from females, and may have also been related to particular behaviors. For example, male African elephants have tusks, while females do not. These tusks are used during combat or jousting with other males. Male deer use antlers to wrestle with rivals to win the favor of females during the mating season.

Suggested sexual dimorphism has been observed in at least three kinds of ornithopods.

One of the earliest ornithopods, *Heterodontosaurus*, is usually found with a quartet of tusklike teeth in its jaws. Another heterodontosaurid specimen, however, has been found with an identical skull, except that it lacked the tusks. It has been suggested that the tusks were only found in males, although the tuskless variety may have also been a juvenile whose tusks had not yet formed.

The basal ornithopod *Hypsilophodon* shows variation in the spine that may denote an anatomical difference between males and females. In this case, the number of vertebrae fused to the pelvis, known as sacrals, may be either five or six, and varies from individual to individual. This is a highly unusual occurrence because the number of sacral vertebrae is usually the same for all members of a taxon. It has been suggested that this is the result of sexual dimorphism.

Among hadrosaurs, scientists have discovered an abundance of flamboyant skulls that help distinguish species of duckbill from one another. These same skulls may demonstrate traits associated with male and female members of the same species. Specimens of *Parasaurolophus* have been found with short and long versions of their elaborate head crest, suggesting a gender difference as the cause. Dodson made a case for sexual dimorphism in *Lambeosaurus* based on numerous specimens with otherwise identical skeletal elements.

Eggs, Nests, and Parental Care in Ornithopods

Dinosaurs hatched from eggs, like their bird descendants and most living reptiles. Hundreds of dinosaur egg sites have been discovered; three-quarters of these are in North America and Asia. Most of the sites that have been found date from the Late Cretaceous Epoch, and many are associated with hadrosaurs. Knowledge of the lifestyle and behavior of ornithopod dinosaurs has been greatly enriched by the discovery of their fossilized eggs, nests, and young. This is largely due to the pioneering work of paleontologist John "Jack" Horner (b. 1946) of the Museum of the Rockies in Montana. Together with his students and colleagues from Montana State University, Horner has spent much of the past 30 years studying the stunning remains of eggs, nests, and skeletons found at numerous fossil sites in northwestern Montana.

We know from these discoveries that at least some kinds of ornithopods nested in colonies and probably took care of their young until they were able to leave the nest on their own. Many of these eggs and nests belonged to *Maiasaura*, so-named "good mother lizard" because of evidence that these duckbill dinosaurs cared for their young. Their behavior is strikingly similar to that in modern birds.

From 1978 to 1983, Horner and his colleagues unearthed a bonanza of *Maiasaura* eggs and babies. Dating from about 80 million years ago in the Late Cretaceous Epoch, the team had discovered three nesting sites collectively consisting of 14 nests, 42 eggs, and 31 babies. Larger specimens of *Maiasaura* at various stages of growth were also found.

After "discovering" a coffee can full of baby dinosaur bones in a small Montana rock shop in 1978, Horner and his team went into the field to locate more evidence of these dinosaurs. The first dig resulted in the discovery of a hadrosaur nest with the remains of 15 three-foot-long (0.9 m) duck-billed dinosaurs still inside. The work of a few days expanded steadily over the course of a few years as the team continued to discover nests, eggs, and the remains of hadrosaurs of different sizes.

The eggs were laid in bowl-shaped nests about 6.5 feet (2 meters) across and 2.5 feet (0.75 m) deep. An adult hadrosaur—most likely the mother—may have dug out the nest in mud with her hind feet and shaped it into a mound with her forelimbs and muzzle. The hollowed-out mound of mud was then covered with vegetation such as pine needles to protect and incubate the eggs. There were up to 20 eggs per nest. Most puzzling was the fact that the eggs were always found in tiny fragments and with no obvious pattern to their arrangement. It was as if they had been trampled underfoot repeatedly for a long period of time, which is exactly what Horner concluded. This became obvious when the scientists took a close look at the bones of the babies that were found in the nest. The baby dinosaurs found were sometimes up to 3 feet (0.9 m) long. Horner noted two intriguing features of the skeletons that have been interpreted in different ways. The teeth of the young were well worn but the joints in their legs were weak, suggesting to Horner that the baby dinosaurs were eating but were not capable of leaving the nest to fend for themselves. It became apparent to Horner that the hadrosaur babies remained in the nest for an extended period, perhaps as long as eight or nine months. The implication is that an adult dinosaur was looking out for the well being of the babies. Horner pictured an adult dinosaur looking over the nest, protecting the babies from predators, and bringing food for them to eat, in the same fashion that birds care for their young. The reason why crushed eggshells littered the floor of the nest also seemed obvious, for that's what would happen if baby dinosaurs were trampling them for months at a time.

Fossil nesting sites reveal possible parental behavior of *Maiasaura*.

Horner's portrait of hadrosaur family life was made even more compelling by the fact that the nests themselves were part of a larger nesting ground. The nests were spaced about 23 feet (6.9 m) apart, which is about equal to the estimated average length of an adult *Maiasaura*. This suggested that the dinosaurs nested together and made room for an entire herd in a manner similar to bird colonies today. Horner's team also found several deposits of nests and eggs in different layers of rock at the same site, strongly suggesting that the dinosaurs returned to the same spot to lay their eggs more than once. This led Horner to picture a large herd of migrating *Maiasaura*, perhaps 10,000 strong, making their way back to the same nesting grounds year after year.

Horner's interpretation of the *Maiasaura* evidence was not accepted by all. Because no *Maiasaura* embryo has yet been found inside an intact fossil egg, some believe that some of Horner's tiniest "hatchlings" may actually be unhatched embryos. This would explain their extremely small size and undeveloped leg joints. Even the evidence of worn teeth in Horner's *Maiasaura* babies does not prove with certainty that the specimens were not embryos. Horner himself discovered the embryonic remains of another duckbill, *Hypacrosaurus*, that showed tooth wear prior to being hatched.

RADIATION OF THE ORNITHOPODS

Sauropods were the dominant herbivorous dinosaurs of the Jurassic Period. The dwindling of sauropods in the Northern Hemisphere during the Cretaceous Period has been attributed to the rise of flowering plants, for which sauropods may have been poorly equipped to eat, and to the success of various ornithopods.

Iguanodontids and hadrosaurs developed some of the most sophisticated and adaptable dental apparatuses ever seen in plant-eating vertebrates. They were well-equipped for eating the tough stalks and leaves of gymnosperms that remained common in most ecosystems, but equally adept at consuming the softer angiosperms. The secret to these ornithopods' success apparently lay in the mouth, where they evolved a self-sharpening battery of grinding teeth to pulverize their food before it entered the digestive tract.

Sauropods, on the other hand, never developed teeth for chewing. They continued to rely on a process that required them to swallow their food whole, after which it was probably fermented in a capacious gut.

Just why sauropods may not have been able to adapt to eating softer flowering plants is not entirely understood, but it may have had to do with their teeth and eating habits which relied on stripping the stems and branches of ferns, cycads, bennettitaleans, and gymnosperm trees of their fibrous leaves and needles. As the flowering plants diversified and radiated, so too did the ornithopods adapted to eating them. Sauropods may have declined because of a diminishing supply of their favorite foods and competition from herds of ornithopods which were no doubt voracious and well-adapted herbivores.

SUMMARY

This chapter explored the iguanodonts and the hadrosaurids, two of the major families of Cretaceous ornithischian dinosaurs.

1. The clade Ornithischia was a natural group of dinosaurs sharing a common ancestor. All ornithischians were herbivorous and either bipedal or quadrupedal.

2. The Cerapoda is a subgroup of Ornithischia that consists of the additional subgroups Ornithopoda (which in turn includes basal forms and Iguanodontia) and Marginocephalia (which includes Ceratopsia or horned dinosaurs and Pachycephalosauria, the bone-headed dinosaurs).

3. Generally speaking, the evolution of iguanodontians involved an increase in size, increasingly robust adaptations to their plant-grinding jaws and teeth, reduction of their hind toes from four to three, the acquisition of an increasingly quadrupedal stance, and the progressive stiffening of the tail.

4. Hadrosaurs were the last significant group of ornithopods to evolve. They were equipped with complex dental batteries and some had elaborate crests on their heads.

5. The most detailed knowledge of ornithopod sexual dimorphism, growth rates, nesting patterns, and possible parental care is derived from studies of hadrosaurs.

6. In the Cretaceous, large iguanodontians (including hadrosaurs) displaced sauropods as the dominant herbivores in the Northern Hemisphere.

6

HORNED AND BONE-HEADED DINOSAURS

One of the most familiar images in the folklore of dinosaurs is a battle to the death between *Tyrannosaurus* and the horned dinosaur *Triceratops* (Late Cretaceous, western North America). Triceratops was a large horned dinosaur, one of the last of its kind, and probably would have made a formidable foe for *T. rex* had the theropod been careless enough to engage it in a tussle. Weighing as much as 6 tons (5.4 tonnes), a defensive-minded *Triceratops* had many advantages to draw upon in battle. Its low-profile, stocky body stood on powerful limbs that were stabilized by large, broad, hooflike, four-toed feet. Unlike ornithopods, which had long tails that they used to maintain balance, *Triceratops* had a tail that was short, flexible, and probably of no consequence in maintaining balance. This massive horned dinosaur was naturally surefooted and so did not need its tail for balance.

Whereas most dinosaurs had four or five sacral vertebrae, *Triceratops* had 10, all the more to fortify its shock-absorbing vertebral column when the animal engaged in fending off predators or locking horns with rivals of its own kind. The business end of *Triceratops* was the enormous skull, measuring up to 8 feet (2.4 m) long and equipped with stout horns over the eyes and a shorter, broader horn on the nose. The perimeter of its skull was adorned with a bony extension called a frill and it protected the area behind the head. The anterior end of the neck, where it supported the heavy skull, was made up of four fused vertebrae to provide extra support and strength. *Triceratops* was nothing less than a living tank and it

Triceratops

can be assumed that predatory dinosaurs rarely took a chance by attacking a healthy adult of this horned dinosaur.

Triceratops is the most familiar member of the Ceratopsia, a subgroup within the clade of Cerapoda termed Marginocephalia, or "bordered heads." Marginocephalians were a group of ornithischian dinosaurs that included the Ceratopsia ("horned faces") and Pachycephalosauria ("thick-headed lizards"). The name Marginocephalia refers to a bony shelf at the back of the skull that is characteristic of all members of the clade. In ceratopsians such as *Triceratops*, this bony shelf was expanded, often enormously, to compose the frill. In pachycephalosaurs, sometimes called bone-headed dinosaurs, the shelf was less pronounced but always accompanied by a thick skull cap from which this clade gets its name.

All marginocephalians were herbivores. Ceratopsians ranged in length from about 3.3 feet (1 m) in the most basal members to nearly

30 feet (9 m) in the largest taxa such as *Triceratops*. Except for a few primitive forms such as *Yinlong* (Late Jurassic, China), *Psittacosaurus* (Early Cretaceous, central and eastern Asia), *Chaoyangsaurus* (Late Jurassic or Early Cretaceous, China), and *Liaoceratops* (Early Cretaceous, China), the horned dinosaurs were obligate quadrupeds. The pachycephalosaurs, whose domed skull cap was up to several inches thick in some taxa, were small to medium-sized bipedal herbivores measuring up to 15 feet (4.5 m) long.

This chapter explores the evolution and lifestyles of the Marginocephalia.

THE CERATOPSIA (HORNED DINOSAURS)

The characteristics outlined above for *Triceratops* were typical of the most derived members of the clade Ceratopsia. The roots of the ceratopsians can be traced to the Late Jurassic and Early Cretaceous Epochs, when their small, predominantly bipedal ancestors such as *Yinlong, Chaoyangsaurus,* and *Psittacosaurus* lived. All other ceratopsians were part of the larger group Neoceratopsia, which is further divided into two clades: the Protoceratopsidae, a group of basal neoceratopsians, and Ceratopsidae, the large-bodied horned dinosaurs. All ceratopsians shared the following features: a rostral bone and beak at the tip of the snout; flaring, bony cheeks, often adorned with a hornlet or spike; an elevated roof of the mouth; and a frill on the back of the skull, albeit small in the most primitive taxa. Having an obvious nose horn or brow horns is not a requirement for being a member of the horned dinosaurs, although even the apparently hornless taxa, such as *Psittacosaurus* and *Protoceratops,* have large cheek horns that jut from the sides of their skulls.

Basal Ceratopsians

The most primitive members of the Ceratopsia are represented by *Yinlong,* a group called the Chaoyangsauridae, the Psittacosauridae, and a number of basal members of the Neoceratopsia, most notably the protoceratopsids. Most basal Ceratopsia have been found in

Asia, whereas the larger, more derived horned dinosaurs all hail from western North America.

Yinlong ("hidden dragon") is a basal ceratopsian from the Late Jurassic Epoch of China. It was small and primarily bipedal, measuring only 4 feet (1.2 m) long. It is currently the oldest known member of the ceratopsians. Its skull features a bony ridged cap also seen in early pachycephalosaurs as well as a small but well-defined frill that is characteristic of horned dinosaurs.

Psittacosauridae consists of only one undisputed taxon, *Psittacosaurus* ("parrot lizard"), which is represented by at least 10 named species—probably not all of which are valid—and multiple specimens of complete skeletons of individuals in various stages of growth. *Protoceratops* ("first horned face"), an equally important early neoceratopsian, was a small quadruped with a short frill. Both of these dinosaurs were discovered in 1923, during an expedition to Mongolia by a team from the American Museum of Natural History.

Until recently, scientific understanding of the most primitive ceratopsians barely extended beyond what is known of *Psittacosaurus* and *Protoceratops*. With the exception of a few intermittent finds, research on basal ceratopsians progressed at a slow pace between 1923 and the 1990s and the start of new explorations in China. Since that time, paleontologists working on the earliest horned dinosaurs have been uncovering remarkable new specimens from Early Cretaceous deposits, some of which have also yielded feathered dinosaurs, filling in gaps and introducing new puzzles to the story of ceratopsian evolution.

The origin of ceratopsians appears to be firmly rooted in Asia. Ceratopsians represent a monophyletic group with a single common ancestor. *Psittacosaurus* is widely regarded as one of the most primitive ceratopsians, but was probably a sister group to the Neoceratopsia rather than their common ancestor. The biggest psittacosaurs were only about 6.5 feet (2 meters) long, including the tail. They weighed about as much as a German shepherd. The psittacosaur skull is notable for its parrotlike beak. The small skull had a boxy shape when viewed from the side and was composed mainly of thin, delicate bones with large openings for the eye and behind the eye. This beak was a forerunner of that seen in neoceratopsians. The cheek area of the skull was reinforced by thickened bony points that would be retained in all later certatopsians.

Psittacosaur teeth were positioned in the cheek area like those of other ceratopsians but were more widely spaced and had rounded, ridged tops for cutting and grinding vegetation. In contrast, the horned giants such as *Triceratops* developed complex batteries of teeth whose function was primarily for shredding tough plant material rather than chewing or grinding it.

In psittacosaurs, the characteristic frill of the ceratopsians was only slightly developed; it took the form of a bony ridge around the back of the head that hinted at the large neck frill seen in neoceratopsians. The skull was short and tall, with a high palate in the mouth and the distance from the eye to the front of the skull was proportionately shorter than in any other known dinosaur taxa, giving *Psittacosaurus* a truly parrotlike appearance. Psittacosaurs had five fingers on their hands, although two of these were smaller and weaker.

Discoveries of psittacosaurs have accelerated in recent years. A contentious new genus, *Hongshanosaurus* (Early Cretaceous, China), was proposed in 2005 by Chinese paleontologist Hailu You based on two fossil skulls, one a juvenile. This taxon is reported to have a shorter skull than *Psittacosaurus* as well as an elliptically shaped eye socket. Remarkably, six new species of psittacosaurs have been described since 1997.

In 1999, a primitive horned dinosaur named *Chaoyangsaurus* ("Chaoyang lizard") from China cast some light on the position of *Psittacosaurus* in the evolution of ceratopsians. *Chaoyangsaurus* was dated from the end of the Jurassic Period or the beginning of the Cretaceous. It has some of the anatomical traits seen in both the protoceratopsids and the ceratopsids that came

A *Psittacosaurus* skull

later, and it appears to be a common ancestor to them both. This places *Chaoyangsaurus* within the Neoceratopsia and not with the psittacosaurs.

It was once thought that psittacosaurs were the ancestors of all other horned dinosaurs. The presence of *Chaoyangsaurus* instead suggests that psittacosaurs were a side branch of the Ceratopsia evolutionary tree rather than the direct ancestors of neoceratopsians. Going back even further in time, the deeper roots of all Ceratopsia probably lie with animals such as *Yinlong* from the Late Jurassic of western China, and perhaps even with the Early Jurassic heterodontosaurids. *Chaoyangsaurus* is currently accepted as the most basal Neoceratopsia.

Protoceratopsids were a basal group of the Neoceratopsia, a clade of small, frilled dinosaurs found in Late Cretaceous deposits of China, Mongolia, and North America. The best-known taxa include *Protoceratops* (Late Cretaceous, Mongolia and China) and *Bagaceratops* (Late Cretaceous, Mongolia). Protoceratopsids were small—the largest specimens only measured about 6 feet (1.8 m) long from the beak to the tail. The skulls of *Protoceratops* and its close relatives were also at the small end of the ceratopsian scale, at a maximum of about 22 inches (55 cm) long. The neck frill was pronounced, but short.

Protoceratopsids had stubby claws on their hands and feet and walked primarily on four legs, although they probably could have risen up on two legs if necessary. They had eight fused sacral vertebrae over the hip—an intermediate step from the customary four or five fused vertebrae found in other dinosaurs and the 10 found in the larger, more derived ceratopsians.

The beak of *Protoceratops* was strong and sharp for snipping vegetation. It had teeth in the front of its mouth as well as teeth well inside the mouth, lining the interior of the cheek area. Protoceratopsids may have had large heads because they needed powerful jaws and jaw muscles to chomp the coarse vegetation on which they fed. The tops, or crowns, of the teeth were leaf-shaped with ridges for cutting and slicing plants. Dinosaurs, like other reptiles, always had a new tooth to replace a tooth that was lost. Since *Protoceratops* only had a single replacement tooth resting beneath each exposed tooth, it seems that this dinosaur did not lose its teeth very often.

So many specimens of *Protoceratops* have been discovered that the entire growth cycle of this dinosaur can be studied, from hatchling to adult. The frill developed early in the life of these dinosaurs. The frill had two large holes in it; these holes presumably were covered by skin. By the time *Protoceratops* was about half adult size, the frill took on either a high and wide shape or a low and narrow shape. The difference in shape may have corresponded to which individuals were males and which were females. In addition to the frill, as *Protoceratops* got older, it developed a bony ridge along the center of its skull, beginning at the nose. This ridge may have been used in butting contests between competing males.

The transition from protoceratopsids to the large-frilled centrosaurines and chasmosaurines is represented by several basal neoceratopsians. *Montanoceratops* and *Leptoceratops,* from the Late Cretaceous of Montana and Alberta, represent an important North American transitional phase. This small clade included anatomical features shared with later horned dinosaurs but not with protoceratopsids. These features included a rounded nasal opening, a more elongated shape to the beak and additional changes to the shape of the skull, and more robust feet and digits.

Archaeoceratops (Early Cretaceous, China) was named in 1996 by Dong Zhiming (b. 1937) and represents a small, bipedal ceratopsian that had a small frill, no horn, and measured just 3.33 feet (1 m) long. *Yamaceratops* (Early Cretaceous, Mongolia), described by Peter Makovicky and Mark Norell in 2006, is possibly the most basal taxon to display a number of derived traits traditionally associated with the skulls of classic neoceratopsians. Makovicky and Norell believe that *Yamaceratops* represents an evolutionary stage within the Neoceratopsia between the psittacosaur *Liaoceratops* and *Archaeoceratops.*

There is a remarkable fossil specimen known as the "fighting dinosaurs" that opens a window onto the world of *Protoceratops.* Discovered in Mongolia in 1972, this spectacular find revealed an adult *Protoceratops* locked in mortal combat with the predatory dinosaur *Velociraptor.* The two desert-dwelling dinosaurs were joined in battle at the time of their demise, having been buried alive suddenly by a violent sandstorm or collapsing dune, entangling them forever. The specimen death pose shows the left arm of the predator firmly clenched in the jaws of the struggling *Protoceratops.* The value of this specimen is immeasurable. Not only does it confirm the predator-to-prey relationship between these two animals, but it also offers a glimpse at the kind of life-and-death struggles that probably took place every day in the wide expanses of Cretaceous Asia.

The fighting dinosaurs: *Protoceratops* and *Velociraptor*

Ceratopsidae

The Ceratopsidae were large-bodied horned dinosaurs from the Late Cretaceous of western North America. *Triceratops*, described at the beginning of this chapter, was a typical ceratopsid and exhibited many of the classic traits associated with this clade. No widely accepted evidence of ceratopsid taxa have yet been found below the Equator.

Ceratopsids are further divided into the Centrosaurinae, horned dinosaurs with short frills, and Chasmosaurinae, horned dinosaurs with long frills. Ceratopsids were large and heavy; the longest were about 30 feet (9 m) long.

Ceratopsids had from one to four horns on the nose and brow. In most taxa, there is one horn positioned on the center of the nasal area; however, a new specimen, unearthed in 2006 in Utah by paleontologists Don DeBlieux and Jim Kirkland, had two nasal horns positioned on the centerline of the skull. Some taxa, including *Pachyrhinosaurus* (Late Cretaceous, Alberta and Alaska) and *Achelousaurus* (Late Cretaceous, Montana), had a wide, flattened nasal bump, or "boss," instead of horns—a feature that probably was covered with a thickened skin pad similar to that seen in the modern musk ox.

Horns were not restricted to the noses and brows of these dinosaurs; they were also found in the form of hornlets and longer, straight or curved horns around the perimeter of the frill and adorning the bony cheek area. The same Utah species recently discovered by DeBlieux and Kirkland and yet to be formally named or described may have more horns and hornlets than any previously known species. Kirkland says that—counting the two nasal horns, brow horns, cheek nodes, and all of the hornlets and longer horns lining the perimeter of its large frill—the new ceratopsid had 14 pairs of horns.

The ceratopsid skull, including the frill, made it one of the largest and heaviest known for any terrestrial vertebrate group. The skull of *Torosaurus* (Late Cretaceous, western North America), a typical large-bodied ceratopsian, measured a hefty 6.5 to 9 feet (2.2 to 2.7 m) long. The nasal openings were enlarged and connected to an extended network of nasal passages that may have been used to ventilate the brain in the large head. Ceratopsid skulls included an extra space between the outer wall and the braincase. This probably acted as a shock absorber to protect the brain during head-butting contests between rival males. The "Think About It" sidebar in this chapter offers more information about the form and possible function of ceratopsian horns and frills.

Ceratopsids had well-developed batteries of teeth. Unlike their earlier relatives the psittacosaurs and protoceratopsids—whose teeth were loosely assembled and infrequently replaced—ceratopsids developed sets of tightly packed teeth that could be continually replaced. The teeth were located in the cheek area and configured in columns with as many as four replacement teeth below an exposed tooth at the top of a column. Counting the replacement teeth, an adult *Triceratops* had nearly 600 teeth in its mouth at any given time. The tooth columns butted up against each other to form a long cutting surface. The tops of the teeth were not flat but had a sharp ridge across the surface. When the teeth of the upper and lower jaws came together, they acted as dozens of scissors, shearing away at vegetation caught between the jaws. These teeth were not flat and could not be used for effective chewing or grinding of food. The food was swallowed in chunks, where it was then processed in the gut.

The ceratopsid neck frill was well-developed and often large. It was made of solid bone in some ceratopsids, such as *Triceratops*, but usually had openings in its bony framework in others such as *Chasmosaurus* (Late Cretaceous, Alberta). The openings looked like rounded windows in the bony outline of the frill.

Ceratopsids were quadrupedal. Their hind limbs were firmly positioned in an erect posture underneath their bodies, but their front legs bent out somewhat at the elbows. Their digits were rounded and blunt on both the hands and feet. Ceratopsids probably could trot or gallop on occasion, but could not run as swiftly as a modern rhinoceros, whose front legs are not as sprawling.

The spinal column of ceratopsids was fused in two places. There were four fused vertebrae at the point where the neck connected to the heavy skull and 10 sacral vertebrae providing a strong connection to the pelvic region.

The centrosaurines, or short-frilled ceratopsids, include six accepted taxa and several questionable members. Centrosaurines had shorter frills than the chasmosaurines, and all but the most basal forms such as *Albertaceratops* (Late Cretaceous, Alberta and

Montana) had long nasal horns. The longest nose horn for a centro-saurine was found in *Styracosaurus* (Late Cretaceous, Alberta) and measured about 24 inches (60 cm). Note that this measurement is for only for the fossilized core of the horn. In the living creature, the horn would have been covered with a horny sheath and therefore several inches longer. The centrosaurines were generally smaller

THINK ABOUT IT

Ceratopsian Horns and Frills

The evolution of highly specialized, increasingly robust and varied horns and frills in ceratopsians begs the question of their utility and function. No one doubts that horns and frills were used for protection. The ceratopsian frill provided protection for the neck, normally one of the most vulnerable parts of the body to be targeted by predators. Horns on the nose and brow were undoubtedly dangerous weapons when thrust into action by an angry ceratopsian. Why, however, was there such a great variety in the morphology of frills and horns? Why did some ceratopsids have brow horns and others nasal horns? Why were horns often curved up or even down? What was the purpose of the elaborate scallops, knobs, and spikes that adorned the frills of many of these dinosaurs? Paleontologists discuss several secondary reasons for the development of such horns and frills in the ceratopsians.

Frills and jaws. Frills may have provided additional surface area for the attachment of jaw muscles. Some paleontologists have thought that such muscles were long and stretched onto the wide, flat area of the top surface of the frill. This would have required a set of jaw muscles nearly 5 feet (1.5 meters) long in a dinosaur such as *Torosaurus*. Because increasing the length of a muscle does not make it stronger, however, and other equally large plant-eating dinosaurs did not find it necessary to evolve such long jaw muscles, it is more likely that the jaw muscles were attached to the base of the frill and no further.

than the chasmosaurines. Their body length ranged from about 13 to 23 feet (4 to 7 m) long. With some exceptions, centrosaurine brow horns were usually greatly reduced but their frills were elaborately adorned with spikes, bony knobs, and distinctive outlines. Representative centrosaurines included *Achelousaurus, Centrosaurus* (Late Cretaceous, Alberta), *Einiosaurus* (Late Cretaceous, Montana),

Visual display. The frills of the horned dinosaurs varied widely from individual to individual within the same species. The study of the various stages of growth of ceratopsians has also shown that the frill grew large and prominent when the animals reached sexual maturity. This fact alone suggests that frills, and horns as well, were not meant purely for defensive purposes because an animal lived for most of its youth without them. Frills also may have figured prominently in attracting members of the opposite sex. Perhaps the largest and most decorative frills were viewed as belonging to the most desirable mates. Large and prominent frills also may have been colored or arrayed with various studs, spikes, and bony plates. When the animal was viewed face to face, the frill probably made the dinosaur look much bigger. In addition to attracting a mate, this visual display could have been used to intimidate a predator or even another rival horned dinosaur. Lowering the head and shaking the frill from side to side might have served as a challenge or a warning to stay away.

Social combat. The male members of several kinds of modern horned animals often use their weaponry in head-to-head competition with rival males. These animals are not trying to kill each other but rather are testing each other, either to establish or maintain dominance in their herd's social hierarchy. It is possible that horned dinosaurs also behaved in this way. They may have locked nasal horns and swung their heads from side to side or butted each other to gain dominance. There is even some evidence of skull wounds because of the accidental stabbing of one male horned dinosaur by another.

Pachyrhinosaurus, and *Styracosaurus.* Centrosaurines also sported some of the most unusual headgear of all dinosaurs. The forward-pointing nasal horn of *Einiosaurus* ("buffalo lizard") resembled a giant can opener. In addition to a prominent nasal horn, *Styracosaurus* ("spiked lizard") had six sizeable spikes flaring outward from its neck frill.

The chasmosaurines were typically larger than the centrosaurines, spanning a range from 17 to 30 feet (5 to 9 m). The largest may have weighed close to 8.5 tons (7.7 tonnes). All had long, prominent horns over the eyes and a smaller horn on the nose. The longest of these brow horns was that of *Torosaurus* at about 32 inches (80 cm). In life, the horn would have been longer when covered with its keratinous sheath. Representative members of the chasmosaurines were *Eotriceratops* (Late Cretaceous, Alberta), *Triceratops, Torosaurus, Chasmosaurus,* and *Pentaceratops* (Late Cretaceous, New Mexico).

Safety in Numbers

Although trackway evidence is not widespread for ceratopsians, there is abundant evidence that horned dinosaurs traveled in large groups or herds. Extensive bone beds, often with a jumble of 100 or more skeletons of juveniles and adults, have been found for *Anchiceratops* (Late Cretaceous, Alberta), *Chasmosaurus, Centrosaurus, Pachyrhinosaurus,* and *Styracosaurus.* This suggests that ceratopsids gathered in large herds and possibly migrated.

An extensive bone bed of *Centrosaurus* was discovered in 1977 in Dinosaur Provincial Park in Alberta, Canada. The bone bed includes the remains of 300 to 400 individuals ranging from young to old. Those individuals were probably once part of an even greater herd that had tried to cross a flood-swollen river. Many of them drowned in the crossing. Their bodies were washed downstream and accumulated along the river bed, where they eventually became fossilized. The presence of shed theropod teeth at the site suggests that scavenging predatory dinosaurs picked over the bodies before they were buried.

THE PACHYCEPHALOSAURIA (BONE-HEADED DINOSAURS)

The Pachycephalosauria ("thick-headed lizards") consisted of small to medium-sized bipedal, ornithischian herbivores that measured in length up to about 15 feet (4.5 m). They are the only dinosaur group distinguished by a thick, bony skull cap. Of the 14-plus recognized genera of pachycephalosaurs, nine are known only from skulls and skull fragments. Only a single new taxon of pachycephalosaur has been named in the past 25 years (*Sphaerotholus*, in 2002), indicating the relative scarcity of this clade in the fossil record of dinosaurs.

Pachycephalosauria are classified as a clade within the Marginocephalia and taxonomically defined as marginocephalians that are more closely related to *Pachycephalosaurus* than to *Triceratops*. The clade is further divided into two subgroups: the Homalocephaloidea, a more primitive taxa that had flattened heads, and the Pachycephalosauridae, having a prominent domelike skull cap. Recent studies have suggested, however, that the distinction between flattened and domed heads might merely be related to the age of the animal, the domed head being fully formed only after reaching sexual maturity. Most pachycephalosaurs have been found in North America, Europe, and Asia and lived from the Early to Late Cretaceous Epochs.

In addition to having thick, bony caps, the skulls of the Pachycephalosauria were ornamented in several unusual ways. *Stegoceras* (Late Cretaceous, western North America), *Prenocephale* (Late Cretaceous, Mongolia), and the recently discovered *Sphaerotholus* (Late Cretaceous, Montana and New Mexico) had a marginal ridge with bony knobs at the base of the dome in the rear of the skull. *Homalocephale* (Late Cretaceous, Mongolia and China) had a flat head with bony knobs on top and a similar margin of bony nodules around the back of the skull, plus small horns pointing to the rear over the neck. *Stygimoloch* (Late Cretaceous, western North America) had a bit of everything: a rounded skull cap, bony spikes on its nose, a protective row of bony knobs over its eyes, and several pairs of formidable spikes jutting up from the back of the head behind its ears. The various knobs and spikes adorning their skulls were probably also important ways for pachycephalosaurs to tell one individual from another and to display one's prowess to members of the opposite sex.

It is widely assumed that the domed head of the pachycephalosaurs was used for head-butting with other individuals. The same kind of behavior can be seen today in bighorn sheep. They square off and repeatedly butt heads with all of their might until one male is forced to give up and back off. Pachycephalosaurs may have done the same, squaring off with their battering-ram skulls, running headlong into each other. Because the skull cap of these dinosaurs was rounded and small, however, some paleontologists doubt whether head-butting was common among pachycephalosaurs. They would have had to have great aim to make it work. Otherwise, their heads would have just glanced off of each other. Instead, these dinosaurs may have used their heads to ram against the side of a rival, a contest that might have been a little less jarring to the brain. The backbones of pachycephalosaurs had a tightly packed, interlocking structure that was well-made to absorb the shock of such contests, and their legs were strong enough to propel them forward with considerable power. Their shock-absorber necks allowed them to engage in head- and thigh-banging contests with little danger of permanent injury.

The bipedal posture of pachycephalosaurs was aided by a spine that locked the vertebrae together for strength and flexibility. The animals walked in a leaning position, with their back parallel to the ground. Because the upper part of the pachycephalosaur leg (the **femur**) was longer than the lower part (the **tibia** and fibula), these dinosaurs were probably not fast runners.

Pachycephalosaurs had teeth and eating habits that were most similar to those of the armored and plated dinosaurs. Pachycephalosaurs were not very tall, so they probably browsed on plants only a meter or so above the ground. Their teeth were divided into two basic groups. The small front teeth were sharp and could grasp and tear plants. The rear teeth were positioned in the cheeks and had triangular ridges for shredding vegetation. These animals were able to pluck and puncture leaves and small fruits with their front teeth and shred them with their cheek teeth. Their wide rib cage suggests that the bone-headed dinosaurs had a large gut for fermenting swallowed food.

The pachycephalosaur *Stegoceras* ("roofed horn") is known from more fossil remains than all other members of the clade. More than two dozen skulls and skull fragments have been found for this dinosaur. Paleontologist Ralph Chapman conducted a study of the skulls and found that they could be divided into two groups: those with a thick-walled dome and those with a thinner dome. He concluded that the ones with the thicker domes were males because of the belief that they used their heads to butt rival males.

MARGINOCEPHALIA SUCCESS

Ceratopsians and other marginocephalians were highly abundant animals. They represent about one-quarter of the dinosaur taxa discovered from the latest Cretaceous Period. Together with the iguanodontian ornithopods, these dinosaurs successfully displaced sauropods as the dominant large herbivores in the Northern Hemisphere. Like the success of the ornithopods during the same time, marginocephalians may have succeeded where sauropods failed in adapting to the consumption of a more diverse vegetarian diet that included both tough-skinned gymnosperms and the softer flowering plants that were rapidly spreading during the Late Cretaceous.

Unlike ornithopods, ceratopsians did not posses teeth designed to chew and pulverize their food before swallowing it—a limitation also seen in sauropods. A question therefore remains as to why horned dinosaurs were better adapted to eating angiosperms than were sauropods. Analogies from living reptiles and mammals help to understand how the ceratopsian digestive system may have worked.

Extant reptiles, none of which chew their food before swallowing it, digest the contents of their stomach slowly. It appears that ceratopsians were somewhat similar. Even the later horned dinosaurs, with their extensive sets of teeth, were unable to chew their food very well before swallowing it. They must have had a powerful digestive system to process the food. After dicing up vegetation with their teeth, a ceratopsian swallowed the shreds and passed them into the gut, where they were digested and fermented to extract nutrients. The stomach must have been adapted to squeeze every ounce of nutrition from the unchewed plant material. Like an elephant, perhaps a ceratopsian only fully digested about 40 percent or 50 percent of what it ate, the rest being too tough to process. A diet consisting more of soft leaves and stems, available to the last of the ceratopsians, would have been easier to digest. While this approach to processing food might work on the scale of a ceratopsian, it does not appear to work for larger animals such as the enormous sauropods, for which it would have been impossible to consume enough food to sustain their metabolism if only 40 percent or 50 percent of it could be digested.

Interestingly, there is evidence that *Psittacosaurus* may have had additional help in digesting its food. Several specimens of this dinosaur have been found with gastroliths, or "stomach stones," associated with the gut area. These small stones may have been swallowed by the dinosaur and used in the stomach to help grind up plant material. Although definitive gastroliths have yet to be found with any other ceratopsian, it is possible that other members of this clade employed them as well.

SUMMARY

This chapter explored the evolution and lifestyles of the Marginocephalia.

1. The Marginocephalia were ornithischian dinosaurs that included the Ceratopsia ("horned faces") and Pachycephalosauria ("thick-headed lizards'). They were a subgroup of the Cerapoda, the same group that included the ornithopods.

2. The name Marginocephalia refers to a bony shelf at the back of the skull that is characteristic of all members of the clade.

3. Marginocephalia are found only in the Northern Hemisphere and probably had origins in Asia.

4. The roots of the ceratopsians can be traced to the Late Jurassic and Early Cretaceous and their small, bipedal early representatives such as *Yinlong, Chaoyangsaurus,* and the Psittacosauridae. All other ceratopsians were part of the larger group Neoceratopsia, which is further divided into the Protoceratopsidae, a group of basal neoceratopsians, and Ceratopsidae, the large-bodied horned dinosaurs.

5. The most primitive members of the Ceratopsia are represented by *Yinlong, Chaoyangsaurus,* the Psittacosauridae, and a number of basal members of the Neoceratopsia, most notably the protoceratopsids.

6. Ceratopsids—the horned dinosaurs—included the Centrosaurinae, horned dinosaurs with short frills, and Chasmosaurinae, horned dinosaurs with long frills. Ceratopsids were large and heavy, the largest being about 30 feet (9 meters) in length.

7. The ceratopsid skull, including the frill, made it one of the largest and heaviest known for any terrestrial vertebrate.

8. Ceratopsian frills likely provided several functions: as a defensive shield against predators or rivals, an attachment point for jaw muscles, and a visual display device for recognizing individuals, attracting a mate, or intimidating rivals.

9. The Pachycephalosauria consisted of small to medium-sized bipedal ornithischian herbivores measuring from about 2 to 15 feet (0.6 to 4.5 meters) in length. They are the only dinosaur group distinguished by a thick, bony skull cap.

SECTION FOUR:
MESOZOIC SEAS AND SKIES

PTEROSAURS: FLYING REPTILES OF THE MESOZOIC ERA

The first vertebrates to achieve powered flight were the Pterosauria, the "winged lizards." Their rise and success paralleled that of the dinosaurs and lasted as long. Pterosaurs mastered the air in many forms and ranged in size from that of a small bird to the largest vertebrate ever to soar through the skies, *Quetzalcoatlus* (Late Cretaceous, Texas), a creature with a wingspan of 40 feet (12 m).

Pterosauria, the flying reptiles, were *not* dinosaurs. They were also not related to birds. All dinosaurs were more closely related to birds than were the pterosaurs. The fact that pterosaurs and birds had the ability to fly is a good example of convergent evolution. Convergent evolution explains that different kinds of animals, although evolutionarily unrelated, often adapt to comparable environments by evolving similar anatomical traits.

Although pterosaurs were not dinosaurs, they probably shared a common ancestor with the dinosaurs from which their evolution quickly diverged in the Late Triassic, the same time as the rise of the first dinosaurs. Within the Archosauria, pterosaurs were the closest major sister group to dinosaurs and shared the planet as masters of the air until the great mass extinction at the end of the Cretaceous Period that also claimed non-avian dinosaurs and marine reptiles as victims. In total, there are about 60-plus known taxa of pterosaurs. This chapter explores the rise and diversification of these animals.

EVOLUTION OF THE PTEROSAURS

Pterosaurs were discovered many years before the term *dinosaur* became a household word. The first scientific description of a pterosaur fossil was written in 1784 for a specimen discovered in Germany. The specimen was found in the limestone quarries of Solnhofen, the same general area in which *Archaeopteryx*, the first bird, was discovered more than 75 years later. The pterosaur in question was *Pterodactylus* (Late Jurassic, Germany); however, it was not named until 1812, when French anatomist Georges Cuvier (1769–1832) ascertained that the fossil represented a form of extinct reptile that was previously unknown. Cuvier named it *Pterodactylus* ("wing finger") after the long fourth finger that made up much of the length of the wing. The animal had a long, toothed snout and a wingspan of about 30 inches (76 cm).

The wonderfully preserved fossils from the limestone quarries of Solnhofen continued to reveal new specimens of pterosaurs. By 1847, with the discovery of the first known pterosaur with a long tail—*Rhamphorhynchus* ("beak snout")—it was clear that two basic forms of pterosaur existed. Some had short tails and some had long tails. Pterosaurs with long tails were part of an informal group called Rhamphorhynchoidea, and they reigned from the Late Triassic Epoch to the Late Jurassic Epoch. The short-tailed variety were part of a group called Pterodactyloidea, and they existed from the Late Jurassic to the Late Cretaceous and were the last pterosaurs to become extinct. The remains of pterosaurs have been discovered on every continent.

Many pterosaurs evidently did not compete directly with dinosaurs for either food or living space. Studies of their habitats and feeding specializations suggest that pterosaurs typically filled a role in the environment as fish-eaters or possible scavengers, living on cliffs and other out-of-the-way places where dinosaurs did not tread. This is not to say that the dinosaurs and pterosaurs did not ultimately compete for survival. The extinction of the smaller

Pterodactylus and *Rhamphorynchus*

pterosaurs may have been catalyzed by a new kind of dinosaur that arose near the end of the Age of Dinosaurs: the smaller, quicker, and probably smarter birds. There is also fossil evidence that some pterosaurs suffered the attacks of predatory dinosaurs. In 2004, paleontologist Eric Buffetaut described the remains of a pterosaur from Africa that included a broken tooth of a spinosaur embedded in the neck.

Because pterosaur remains are typically rare and fragmentary, the taxa we know about are probably only a fraction of those that existed. This lack of information also leads to an oversimplification of pterosaur ecology. While it is true that many pterosaurs seem to have been seagoing or lake-dwelling fish-eaters, there were also small, insectivorous, forest-dwelling pterosaurs (*Anurognathus, Jeholopterus, Nemicolopterus*); shellfish-eating pterosaurs (*Dsungaripterus*); and filter-feeding pterosaurs (*Ctenochasma, Pterodaustro*).

Paleontologist Matt Lamanna says that he would not be surprised if, one day, "somebody found flightless pterosaurs, and herbivorous pterosaurs."

Pterosaur Origins

The origins of the pterosaurs and their flight adaptations are not well understood because of a dearth of fossil evidence of transitional creatures that may have been their ancestors. Such a creature would probably have started to evolve longer front legs than hind legs as a step in the development of wings. An early stage of this evolution may have been a tree-climbing archosaur that developed a wing membrane for gliding. Pterosaurs were not gliders, but a gliding ancestor may have been a step along the way to the evolution of wings for powered flight.

The earliest and most basal pterosaurs, such as *Peteinosaurus* and *Eudimorphodon* from the Late Triassic of Italy, display the kinds of features that might be expected of the least evolved members of the clade. They had oversized, strongly lizardlike heads and short, broad wings that seem like a holdover from an ancestral gliding phase of their evolution. These small rhamphorhynchoids were, nonetheless, powered fliers and provide the best clues to the formative stages of pterosaur evolution.

PTEROSAUR ANATOMY AND ADAPTATIONS

Pterosaurs ranged in size from small, crow-sized creatures with a wingspan of 1 foot (0.3 m) to giants of the sky with wingspans up to 40 feet (12 m)—the size of a small airplane. During their time, pterosaurs were the dominant flying inhabitants of the coastal areas of the world, skimming the oceans for a bounty of fish and invertebrates. They may have lived in great nesting colonies, forming a unique place for themselves in a world otherwise ruled by dinosaurs.

Anatomical features that were common to all pterosaurs included a small body in proportion to the size of the head and limbs. Their skulls were lightweight, heavily windowed, and had large orbits for the eyes. Over time, pterosaur skulls evolved from the tall and short reptilian style of the most basal taxa to long, narrow skulls with elongated jaws and crests. The postcranial bones of pterosaurs were hollow and lightweight. One calculation estimated that a pterosaur with a wingspan of 23 feet (7 m) had a body weight of only about 37 pounds (17 kg).

The powered flight of pterosaurs required specialized bones in the shoulders and breast for the attachment of flight muscles and the reinforcement of wing flapping. The forelimbs making up the wing had four fingers each. The outer halves of the wings were shaped by the fourth digit of each hand. Unlike birds and bats, pterosaurs had one finger of the hand that was lengthened in this way to frame the leading edge of the wing. The three remaining fingers of the forelimbs that were not attached to the wing had curved claws for grasping prey or holding tightly to a vertical perch, such as a cliff wall. Powered flight was aided by a specially shaped breastbone to anchor flight muscles. In later pterosaurs, several of the bones of the upper back were fused together to strengthen the shoulders for flight. The breastbone of pterosaurs was large but not as pronounced as the keel-like breastbone seen in birds.

The pterosaur body was covered in leathery skin, and some specimens show evidence of a hairy or fuzzy body covering that may have been present in all species. The wing membrane consisted of leathery skin reinforced by stiff fibers.

Not all pterosaurs had teeth. When they did, the configuration and size of the teeth was extremely variable depending on the taxon. One thing common to all toothed pterosaurs was that the teeth were always single-rooted and embedded in their own individual sockets within the jaw. The teeth were cone-shaped and did not have a cutting edge, making them primarily useful for snagging prey as the pterosaur flew by. Variation in the configuration of the teeth can be seen in the size and placement of the teeth in the jaw. The teeth of the upper and lower jaws often interlocked when the mouth closed, creating a firm grip on whatever the pterosaur was biting.

Pterosaurs had long, narrow toes on the hind limbs and an ankle that could bend enough so that a pterosaur could walk on the soles of its feet rather than on its toes like dinosaurs and birds. Their hind limbs were generally lightweight and weak and had four clawed toes on each foot. The leg bones were short when compared to the enormous length of the wings, but proportionately about the same size as those of a two-legged dinosaur when compared to the body size.

Further anatomical differences are found in the Pterodactyloidea and the Rhamphorhynchoidea. The rhamphorhynchoids had a long tail with elongated vertebrae, jaws with teeth, a full set of neck ribs, and short wrist bones; and were without fused vertebrae in the upper spine. In contrast, the pterodactyloids had a short tail and some taxa were without teeth. Moreover, pterodactyloids had only two neck ribs, had long wrist bones, and had several fused vertebrae in the upper spine that reinforced the spine and enabled these pterosaurs to grow to enormous sizes.

The leathery wing membrane of pterosaurs extended from the side of the animal and was stretched by the bones of the arm and fourth finger when extended. The wing had at least two sections. The forewing was a small patch of wing stretching between the animal's wrist and its shoulder. The main part of the wing was attached to the side and extended the length of the arm all the way to the outer tip of the fourth finger. The wing was flexible enough to be folded close to the body when the animal was on the ground and at rest.

Some of the small rhamphorhynchoids such as *Dimorphodon* (Early Jurassic, England) and *Sordes* (Late Jurassic, Kazakhstan) had a pronounced wing membrane between their hind legs and tail. Most other pterosaurs, especially the short-tailed kinds, did not have a membrane between their legs, but the wings often extended down the very top of the legs.

Pterosaur Dermal Covering

Unlike most non-avian dinosaurs, which had reptilelike skin composed of nonoverlapping scales, pterosaurs had leathery skin more like that of mammals. From the earliest discoveries of pterosaurs, scientists wondered whether this skin may have been covered with an insulating layer of fur or feathers. Such a coating would have helped the creatures retain body heat, an important advantage for an active flyer. In 1970, a fossil of a small pterosaur provided possible evidence that these creatures had been covered with hair. The specimen in question was the remarkable *Sordes*, a small rhamphorhynchoid from Central Asia. What may have been the evidence of hair appeared as finely patterned impressions in the fossil. *Sordes pilosus* ("hairy devil") seemed to have had furry wings with a dense coat of hairs that were about 0.25 inch (6.35 mm) long.

As interesting as this discovery was, the supposed hair of *Sordes* differed greatly from the kind of hair seen in mammals. The fibers

THINK ABOUT IT

Origins of Powered Flight

Animals can fly using one of three methods: gliding, soaring, and powered flight. Gliding uses large airfoils—wings—to suspend an animal in the air for a slow descent. Soaring uses wings designed to allow a creature to rise and fall on updrafts of air. Wings designed for powered flight require vigorous flapping to stay aloft but may also make some gliding and soaring possible. Some birds, such as gulls and albatrosses, use powered flight for taking off and then soar to remain aloft for long periods.

Insects, bats, birds, and pterosaurs all fly (or in the case of pterosaurs, flew) under their own power. Among animals with backbones, powered flight has evolved three separate times—first in pterosaurs, then in birds, and finally in bats—each independently of one another.

Most modern birds are strong enough to become airborne from a standing start. Just how the pterosaurs took flight may have depended on their size. The smaller pterosaurs, such as *Rhamphorhynchus* and *Pterodactylus*, probably could take off from the ground, like birds, by on the skin of *Sordes* were single, unbranched strands of fiber that did not originate from hair follicles. Nothing like hair had ever been seen before in a pterosaur. In 1994, paleontologists David Unwin and Natalia Bakhurina showed that the traces seen in the *Sordes* specimen were not mammal-like hair at all, but stiffening fibers that probably gave strength to the wings. These same fibers have also been seen in other pterosaurs. So, the "hairy devil" *Sordes* may not have been so hairy after all. Nevertheless, fossil evidence for some sort of hair or fuzz has now been seen in nine pterosaur specimens from various localities and time periods. Unwin recently wrote that this is "a strong hint that most, if not all, of these Mesozoic dragons were hairy."

flapping their wings. The larger pterosaurs, including *Pteranodon* (Late Cretaceous, western North America) and *Quetzalcoatlus*, were possibly too heavy to take off without assistance from a strong headwind or a high spot from which to jump.

Taking Wing for the First Time

Because there is so little fossil evidence of likely pterosaur ancestors, there is little debate about the origin of flight in these flyers. Being the first known vertebrates with truly powered flight, they evolved from an earlier form of flightless reptile. It is generally accepted that pterosaurs arose from a line of small reptiles that developed primitive wings in the form of skin membranes. These skin membranes allowed them to glide down from trees, or between trees. As they became more skilled at gliding, turning their bodies and membranes to steer themselves and control their fall, they began to retain anatomical adaptations that eventually came to endow them with powered flight. Over time, these small, active creatures developed increasingly powerful wings along with stronger skeletal structures and muscles to flap them.

Pterosaur Jaws

The oversized skulls of pterosaurs varied widely from one taxon to another. The most typical pterosaur skull shape was long and narrow with a pointed snout, nostrils close to the eyes, and often a dazzling array of pointed teeth for spearing fish. Several others had jaws that were unique even among pterosaurs. The following is an overview of various jaw adaptations found in pterosaurs and representative taxa that possessed such adaptations.

Short, widely spaced, pointed teeth. In some pterosaurs, the teeth in the front of the jaws were usually longer than those in back, enabling the pterosaur to snare fish as it flew over the water. The teeth of the upper and lower jaws might have also meshed when the jaws were closed, providing a firm grip on the prey. Examples of pterosaurs with this kind of teeth were *Eudimorphodon, Dimorphodon,* and *Istiodactylus* (Early Cretaceous, England and China).

Long, angled, widely spaced, needlelike teeth. In these pterosaurs, the front teeth were often long and curved, pointing forward outside of the mouth. Smaller teeth were in the back of the jaws. The front teeth were well-suited for spearing fish. Examples of pterosaurs with these teeth were *Rhamphorhynchus* and *Scaphognathus* (Late Jurassic, Germany).

Peglike, widely spaced teeth and a short, wide jaw. This jaw configuration was best suited for eating insects. The teeth were not angled forward and they could interlock when the mouth was closed. Pterosaurs with this jaw adaptation included *Sordes* and *Anurognathus* ("tail-less jaw").

Long and short, pointed teeth. The teeth of these pterosaurs were longer in the front and angled forward. They were spaced so that they interlocked when the jaws were closed, an advantage for grasping fish. With a mouth full of such teeth, the pterosaur could skim the water to scoop up its prey with ease. Examples were *Pterodactylus* and *Germanodactylus* (Late Jurassic, Germany and France).

Long, closely spaced teeth in the front of the jaws. This jaw adaptation was suited for spearing fish by striking the snout down into the water. Some pterosaurs with this configuration had smaller teeth in the back of the mouth. Examples of pterosaurs using this tooth plan were *Gallodactylus* (Late Jurassic, Germany and France) and *Cearadactylus* (Early Cretaceous, Brazil).

Filterlike basket of teeth. Several pterosaurs had this unusual adaptation on either their lower jaw or both the upper and lower jaws. Long, tightly packed, needle-like teeth acted as a kind of basket around the edge of the mouth. It is unlikely that these creatures fed while they were flying because the force would have damaged their teeth. These pterosaurs probably stood in shallow water like flamingos, bending down to scoop up water in their mouths. By filling its mouth with water, the pterosaur could filter out any small creatures, such a plankton, that were in the water. Examples were *Ctenochasma* (Late Jurassic, France and Germany), *Gnathosaurus* (Late Jurassic, Germany), and *Pterodaustro* (Early Cretaceous, Argentina).

Long, pointed beak with short, pointed teeth in the back of the jaw. This kind of pterosaur may have used its beak to pry open shellfish. Examples of pterosaurs with these teeth included *Dsungaripterus* (Early Cretaceous, China), *Noripterus* (Early Cretaceous, China), and *Phobetor* (Early Cretaceous, Mongolia).

Crested, rudderlike jaws and pointed teeth. These pterosaurs had a mouthful of pointed teeth and a rounded crest on the outside of the top and bottom jaws. When the pterosaur was flying over the water, it could use its rudderlike crested jaws to steady its control in the waves. *Ornithocheirus* (Early Cretaceous, England and Brazil) is an example.

Long, pointed jaws without teeth. Some of the larger pterosaurs had no teeth, using their pointed jaws to grab fish or to scavenge dead animals. Examples were *Pteranodon* and *Quetzalcoatlus*.

Crested Pterosaurs

Many pterosaurs were adorned with bony crests on their heads. These head crests seem to have had two functions. One was that of visual display. Crests were a way to differentiate one individual from another and also to attract the attention of potential mates.

The other function was that of flight stabilization. Several kinds of pterosaur crests were prominent enough to have affected the aerodynamics of the animals' flight.

Crests came in several varieties. One common type was a short, bony ridge running up the center of the snout, a trait seen in many rhamphorhynchoids and pterodactyloids. The purpose of the crest was most certainly for visual display, and the crest may have varied in size between males and females.

Crests on the back of the head were found on many of the pterodactyloids. These crests ranged in size from a small bump such as that on the back of the skull of *Gallodactylus* (Late Jurassic, France), to the long and stunning crests of *Pteranodon*. The latter had two basic crest shapes, each found in a different species. One crest was long and pointed and stretched out behind the head nearly as long as the beak stretched out in front. The other was a wide, hatchet-shaped crest positioned on the cap of the skull, over the eyes. These large crests certainly affected the ability of the animal to maneuver in the air by acting as a kind of rudder for steering and also as counterbalance to the heavy beak. As it was possibly a sexually dimorphic trait, the size of the crest may have differed between males and females.

Several kinds of pterosaurs had a pair of large, rounded crests on the top and bottom of the snout. These semicircular vanes nearly formed a circle when the jaws were closed. It is believed that the pterosaur could dip this crest into the water when it was skimming the sea for food, thereby stabilizing its flight and allowing it to use the water as a medium for changing direction. One could liken this to the action of an oar in the water. *Anhanguera* ("old devil") and *Tropeognathus* ("keel jaw"), from the Late Cretaceous of Brazil, had crests of this variety.

The Braincase

The braincase of a pterosaur skull holds clues to the many connections between the brain and other parts of the body. Evidence of these nerve connections can be seen in the form of holes in the braincase through which nerves were once threaded to attach the brain to other organs.

One of the first scientists to study the structure of brains in extinct creatures was Tilly Edinger. In 1927, she published an important study of the brains of pterosaurs based on casts of their brain cavities. She discovered that pterosaurs had brains that were more like those of modern birds than modern reptiles. This was surprising because, like dinosaurs, pterosaurs evolved from early reptiles. Yet their brains were more like those of birds in their general size, shape, and orientation. The brains of pterosaurs from the Late Jurassic were even more like those of modern birds than was the brain of *Archaeopteryx*, the earliest known bird that lived at the same time as the pterosaurs in question. More recent work by paleontologist Deborah S. Wharton led her to conclude that pterosaurs had brains as well developed as those of modern birds.

One of the most striking differences between pterosaur brains and those of other reptiles is that pterosaur brains have greatly enlarged optic lobes. This makes sense because a flying creature that must swoop down and snatch prey must have superior eyesight.

Pterosaurs evolved a brain that was similar to that of birds because they lived a similar lifestyle. Predatory creatures rely on their senses to locate and catch prey. Animals that fly develop superior senses of balance and vision. The parts of the brain devoted to controlling these abilities, along with steering and maneuvering, were more developed in pterosaur brains than in those of crocodiles, non-avian dinosaurs, and other reptiles. The bird brain evolved in a similar way, emphasizing the development of those parts of the brain devoted to flight, vision, and balance.

Pterosaur Thermoregulation

The question of thermoregulation in dinosaurs has been the source of lively debate, but there is more agreement among paleontologists when it comes to the flying reptiles. From the earliest days of pterosaur study, scientists have concluded that these creatures were **endothermic** (warm–blooded), not **ectothermic** (cold–blooded). Warm-blooded creatures have an internal source of body heat regulated by their heart and circulatory systems. They are not dependent on the environment as their source of heat and can remain physically active for sustained periods of time. Harry Govier Seeley was one of the first great paleontologists to conduct a thorough study of pterosaurs. In 1864, he stated that these flying reptiles were probably warm-blooded. He based his conclusion on the simple fact that a pterosaur's blood would rise in temperature from flapping its wings. To stay aloft, a flying creature needs to flap it wings for long periods of time.

The idea that pterosaurs were warm-blooded is supported by several other pieces of indirect evidence. Their bones show that pterosaurs grew continuously and rapidly, much like today's warm-blooded birds. Perhaps one of the most compelling pieces of indirect evidence for endothermy in pterosaurs has to do with their hollow bones. Like birds, it appears that pterosaurs had a sophisticated network of air sacs connected to their lungs. The air sacs branched throughout the body and even occupied spaces in the hollows of some bones. This had two immediate benefits for a warm-blooded pterosaur. First, it allowed air to circulate throughout the body and keep it cool. Overexertion and overheating are problems for birds and must have been for pterosaurs as well. Second, by recirculating air from the lungs through the bones and back to the lungs again, more oxygen could be absorbed from the air. Muscles need oxygen to work properly, so this respiratory system of air sacs helped the pterosaur utilize its oxygen input most efficiently in support of an endothermic regulatory system. The final piece of evidence in favor of warm-bloodedness in pterosaurs is the fact that many, if not all, of these flying reptiles were covered in hairlike fibers that may have served as insulation, slowing heat loss.

SUMMARY

This chapter explored the rise and diversification of the pterosaurs.

1. The first vertebrates to achieve powered flight were the Pterosauria, the "winged lizards." There are at least 60 known genera of pterosaurs. The remains of pterosaurs have been discovered on every continent.

2. Pterosaurs with long tails were part of an unnatural group called Rhamphorhynchoidea and they reigned from the Late Triassic to the Late Jurassic. The short-tailed variety were part of a group called Pterodactyloidea, and they existed from the Late Jurassic to the Late Cretaceous and included the last pterosaurs to become extinct.

3. The most basal pterosaurs had oversized, lizardlike heads and short, broad wings—possible holdovers from an ancestral gliding phase in their evolution.

4. Pterosaurs ranged in size from small, sparrow-sized creatures with a wingspan of 1 foot (0.3 m) to giants of the sky with wingspans up to 40 feet (12 m), the size of a small airplane.

5. Anatomical traits of all pterosaurs include small bodies, large heads, and a wing whose outer half was formed by an elongated fourth finger of the forelimb.

6. Pterosaurs were probably covered in hairlike filaments.

7. Typical pterosaur teeth were cone-shaped and did not have a cutting edge. Variation in the configuration of the teeth can be seen in the size and placement of the teeth in the jaw.

8. Many pterosaurs had head crests that provided a means of visual display and, in some cases, flight stabilization, serving as a flap or rudder.

9. Pterosaur brains were similar to those of birds and optimized for the senses needed to manipulate flight behavior.

10. Pterosaurs were probably endothermic.

Marine Reptiles of the Mesozoic Era

Marine reptiles were air-breathing creatures that lived in the water. Their ancestors were land-dwelling reptiles from the Permian and Triassic Periods. Except for the marine crocodiles, they were not closely related to dinosaurs. Some marine reptiles trace their ancestry to the roots of the reptilian evolutionary tree, while others were close relatives of lizards and snakes. Like today's turtles and crocodiles, they would hold their breath while under water.

Reptiles first dominated life on land about 300 million years ago, during the late Carboniferous Period. By the end of the Triassic Period, dinosaurs had begun their long stand as masters of the land, while their flying relatives, the pterosaurs, had taken control of the sky. Another group of reptiles took to the sea, where fishes, squids, shelled mollusks, and other sea creatures had long been thriving, nearly unchecked by any significantly larger predatory animals. Fish traveled in huge, silvery schools. Ammonites—soft cephalopod cousins of the squid that lived in coiled shells—propelled themselves through the ocean in large groups, feeding on fishes and other smaller creatures. It is not surprising that some of the highly adaptable reptiles gradually took to the oceans to get their share of this rich bounty of food. Some reptiles gradually returned to the seas sometime in the Permian Period. By the Late Triassic and Jurassic, many surprisingly varied forms of predatory marine reptiles had evolved.

Marine reptiles are grouped in the following categories:

Ichthyosaurs. Tuna- or dolphinlike in appearance, but unrelated to them, ichthyosaurs were one of the most common types of marine reptiles of the Triassic and Jurassic. Ichthyosaurs were the first important reptile group to successfully adapt to marine life. They have been found in many parts of the world and thrived throughout most of the Age of Dinosaurs, though they declined in the Cretaceous Period and likely became extinct before its end. Some were as small as 6 feet (1.8 m) long while others included what was probably the largest ancient marine reptile of all—an ichthyosaur measuring a whopping 77 feet (23 m) long! That's longer than a sperm whale.

Placodonts. These were small to medium-sized, bottom-feeding reptiles that resembled armor-plated walruses. One genus, *Henodus*, bore an astonishingly close resemblance to turtles, though it was not related to them. Placodonts were extinct by the end of the Triassic Period.

Nothosaurs. Streamlined, swift, seal-like predators of the Triassic Period, the nothosaurs and pistosaurs had long necks and tails as well as powerful paddles for swimming. They were probably related to the plesiosaurs, which evolved during the Late Triassic.

Plesiosaurs. These were long- and short-necked open-ocean predators. The long-necked varieties could maneuver quickly to catch fish in their jaws. The short-necked varieties had gaping jaws and were often the top predators in their underwater world. Some of the largest short-necked plesiosaurs, such as *Kronosaurus* and *Liopleurodon*, preyed on any size of animal, including giant sharks.

Marine crocodiles. Several kinds of ocean-going crocodiles evolved during the Mesozoic Era. All are extinct but distantly related to the crocodiles that still exist.

Mosasaurs. These ancient predators had short necks, powerful jaws typically lined with cone-shaped teeth, and long, muscular tails to proper them through the water. Some grew to be more than 33 feet (10 m) long. They have been likened to large, underwater monitor lizards and are thought to be closely related both to these lizards and to snakes.

Marine turtles. These were the first true seagoing turtles. Although they are all extinct, they are related to modern sea turtles.

Marine reptiles were discovered in Europe long before the word *dinosaur* was coined. The skull of *Mosasaurus* ("Meuse River lizard") was discovered in 1780 deep inside a limestone mine in Maastricht, Netherlands. By 1842, when British paleontologist Sir Richard Owen (1804–1892) coined the word *dinosaur*, examples of all the major marine reptile groups had already been described, including mosasaurs, plesiosaurs, ichthyosaurs, nothosaurs, placodonts, marine crocodiles, and marine turtles. In many ways, the study of ancient marine reptiles helped form the foundation of the scientific discipline study that came to be known as vertebrate paleontology—the study of extinct animals with backbones. This chapter provides an overview of the major clades of extinct marine reptiles that lived during the Mesozoic Era.

MARINE REPTILE EVOLUTION

Reptiles had already found success on land when some taxa began to explore the oceans again. Life in the ocean required good swimming skills so that marine reptiles could catch prey and escape predators. Marine reptiles adapted to ocean life by optimizing anatomical traits that reduced drag and provided them with speed and maneuverability in the water. Features such as webbed or flipperlike limbs and a vertical flattening of the tail aided in locomotion and could have also helped them to dive deep. These changes took place gradually over time as terrestrial reptiles took to the ocean.

The fossils of marine reptiles are found mainly in a few well-known locations across the Earth:

- *Triassic marine reptiles (ichthyosaurs, placodonts, nothosaurs):* western Europe (England, France, Germany, Italy, the Netherlands, Spain, Switzerland); United States (California, Nevada, Alaska); Japan; China.
- *Jurassic marine reptiles (ichthyosaurs, pliosaurs, plesiosaurs, marine crocodiles, nothosaurs):* western Europe (England, France, Germany); eastern Europe (Russia); United States (Wyoming); Canada (Alberta, Arctic regions); Argentina; Chile; India; China.

- *Cretaceous marine reptiles (ichthyosaurs, pliosaurs, plesiosaurs, marine crocodiles, marine turtles, mosasaurs):* western Europe (Belgium, England, France, Germany, the Netherlands, Sweden); eastern Europe (Russia); United States (Alabama, Arkansas, California, Colorado, Kansas, Mississippi, Nebraska, New Jersey, South Dakota, Texas, Wyoming); Canada (Manitoba, Saskatchewan); Africa (Angola, Egypt, Niger, Nigeria); Argentina; Brazil; Colombia; Australia (Queensland, South Australia); New Zealand; Antarctica; Japan (Hokkaido).

The most abundant sources of extinct marine reptiles are the western interior of the United States, western Europe, northeast Africa, northeast Australia, and southwestern South America. Each of these areas was the site of a major marine environment sometime during the Mesozoic Era.

THE ICHTHYOSAURS

Ichthyosaurs—the "fish lizards"—were some of the first fossil creatures to attract scientific attention. An illustration of one was published as early as 1699, but the bones were believed to be those of a fish. It was not until 1814 that the renowned French anatomist Georges Cuvier compared the skull and skeletal features of those fossils to the bones of other vertebrates, thereby proving that ichthyosaurs were related to reptiles. This was a startling conclusion to make at the time, during the formative years of the science of paleontology. The name *Ichthyosaurus* (Early Jurassic, England and Germany) was given to all known specimens in 1818 but not published until 1822.

Ichthyosaurs were the first major group of reptiles to adapt to ocean life, but there is little fossil evidence to illustrate the stages of this transformation. It is assumed that ichthyosaurs evolved from a group of land-living reptiles whose legs modified into flippers as they slowly adapted to life in the sea. The discovery of two nearly complete skeletons of an early ichthyosaur in Japan in 1982 finally shed light on the early adaptation of these reptiles to sea life.

Utatsusaurus ("Utatsu lizard") is the earliest known ichthyosaur and dates from the Early Triassic. Before 1982, the only known specimens of this creature were fragmentary and incomplete. The newly discovered skeletons provided paleontologists with their first complete view of an early ichthyosaur. What they discovered revealed much about the evolution of these creatures. Rather than having the distinctly streamlined body found in later ichthyosaurs, *Utatsusaurus* looked more like a typical reptile with flippers. It had a longer, less streamlined body, and its backbone was made up of smaller and longer vertebrae than those found in more derived ichthyosaurs. It appears that early ichthyosaurs such as *Utatsusaurus* moved like eels, undulating their bodies from side to side.

Ichthyosaur remains have been found on every continent except Antarctica and Africa.

Ichthyosaur Anatomy

Ichthyosaurs were the most fishlike in appearance of all marine reptiles, but this resemblance is superficial because the two kinds of animals are not related. The flippers of ichthyosaurs and other marine reptiles are a highly modified form of foot once used to walk on land. The bones are thick and still show the evidence of having once consisted of a wrist or ankle and fingers or toes.

Anatomical traits of ichthyosaurs included:

Streamlined body. Except for the earliest forms, ichthyosaurs had a rounded, streamlined body for swimming through the water with ease. The earliest forms, including *Utatsusaurus, Chaohusaurus* (Early and Middle Triassic, China), and *Cymbospondylus* (Middle Triassic, Germany and Nevada), had longer, more reptilelike bodies with short paddles. The streamlined nature of the body was improved by the animals' having smooth skin rather than the scaly skin of terrestrial reptiles. The first evidence of ichthyosaur skin texture was uncovered by German fossil collector and preparator Bernhard Hauff around 1890.

Specialized backbone. The spine of ichthyosaurs has been described as a row of doubly concave vertebrae the shape of hockey pucks. This unusual design differs from that of most terrestrial reptiles in that it favors locomotion through the water by use of the tail. The ichthyosaurs propelled themselves by waving their large tails from side to side. The hockey-puck design gave the back great flexibility and strength. The earliest known ichthyosaurs from the Triassic Period did not yet have this kind of spine. Their spine was made up of smaller, longer bones that allowed the animal to swim by wriggling its entire body from side to side, like an eel.

Fins. All ichthyosaurs had four side fins—two in front next to the chest (called *forefins*) and two in the rear next to the hip (called *hindfins*). The forefins were always larger than the hindfins. Later ichthyosaurs from the Jurassic also had a dorsal fin on their back, similar to that seen on a shark. Since ichthyosaurs propelled themselves by either undulating the body or waving the tail from side to side, their dorsal and side fins were not used for gaining speed. Instead, fins provided the animal with steering and balance, allowing it to stay upright, go up and down, and make turns. All of these maneuvers would have allowed the animal to control itself even while swimming fast in pursuit of prey.

The forefin became smaller during the course of ichthyosaur evolution. The finger bones became shorter, eventually becoming nearly rectangular. Also, the thumb disappeared midway through ichthyosaur evolution, leaving only four digits. By the end of their evolution, however, ichthyosaurs had developed two additional fingers on the outsides of the original four, which improved the ichthyosaur's ability to swim at high speed in pursuit of prey, further perfecting the fishlike design of these animals over their long history.

Long, tapered skull. Two features dominate the ichthyosaur skull: the large, round eye sockets and the long, narrow jaws. The eyes were enormous in some kinds of ichthyosaurs, often bigger than a grapefruit. Excellent eyesight would have improved the animal's predatory skills and may have also given it the advantage of being able to see in low light conditions.

Jaws and teeth. The long, thin jaws of ichthyosaurs were lined with small, cone-shaped teeth. The animals had as many as 180 to

200 teeth. Except for the earliest ichthyosaurs, these teeth were not implanted in the jawbone but were held in place only by the gums in a long groove. Ichthyosaurs lost and replaced their teeth often. The long jaws were ideally suited for snatching several prey at a time while passing through a group of fleeing fish or floaters such as squid.

Swinging tail. The ichthyosaur tail was vertically oriented, like that of fishes. It was waved from side to side to propel the animal through the water. It also helped stabilize the animal and prevented it from rolling over. Earlier ichthyosaurs from the Triassic Period were less developed in this way. They had flatter, more lizardlike tails with only short tail fins. The tails grew to be more prominent as the ichthyosaurs evolved during the Jurassic Period.

Ichthyosaur Birth

Because the ichthyosaur body was optimized for living full time in the water, like a dolphin's, these animals could not come on land to lay eggs like other reptiles. Ichthyosaurs solved the problem of giving birth by evolving the ability to retain their "eggs" inside the body and give birth to live young when the eggs hatched.

There are a surprising number of fossils illustrating that ichthyosaurs gave birth to live young. Some fossil specimens show several unborn babies in the body cavity of the mother. One remarkable specimen of *Stenopterygius* (Early Jurassic, Germany) preserved an ichthyosaur newborn emerging tail first from the mother's birth canal (as in modern whales), its head still inside the mother. Other specimens show the remains of babies within the body cavity of the mother or in close proximity to the mother after having just been born. Most ichthyosaurs gave birth to one to two young at a time, although as many as 11 have been seen with one specimen.

Ichthyosaur Size

Until recently, the largest known ichthyosaur was a species of *Shonisaurus* (Late Triassic, Nevada) that measured 49 feet (14.7 m) in length. A new, recently discovered species of *Shonisaurus* from British Columbia, however, dwarfs even its American relative. Described in 2004 by Canadian paleontologist Elizabeth Nicholls and Japanese paleontologist Makoto Manabe, the new giant measured about 77 feet (23 m) long, almost twice as long as the previously known record holder. *Shonisaurus* is now the largest of all known marine reptiles.

THE PLACODONTS

Placodonts were relatively small marine reptiles that have been found only in western Europe, Israel, and possibly England. The earliest known taxa lived at the end of the Early Triassic and all were extinct by the end of the Late Triassic. Placodonts measured from 3.5 to 6.5 feet (1 to 2 m) long and would have been dwarfed by some other marine reptiles of the time. Unlike the ichthyosaurs and plesiosaurs, placodonts did not have large paddles or the streamlined body adaptations needed for quick swimming and maneuvering in the water. Their legs were short and stout and barely paddlelike. Their bodies were wide and sometimes armored, and they had little means for accelerating rapidly in the water. Based on their body plan, it is assumed that placodonts lived near the shore and probably moved slowly along the floor of the shallow ocean. Placodonts have been likened in appearance to a combination of a turtle and a walrus.

The first fossil evidence of placodonts consisted of curious black, rounded teeth that were sometimes discovered in limestone quarries in Germany. One collector named Georg Münster took an interest in these "beans," as the quarry diggers called them. In 1830, Münster expressed the opinion that the teeth were from ancient fishes. It wasn't until 1858 that a skull of one of these creatures revealed that they were reptiles and not fish. The first placodonts to be described in great detail were *Placodus* ("flat tooth") and *Cyamodus* ("bean tooth") in 1863, but even these specimens were incomplete. Our understanding of placodonts changed dramatically with the discovery of a complete *Placodus* skeleton from the Middle Triassic of Germany. This extraordinary find provided the missing pieces of the placodont puzzle. Only eight genera of placodonts are widely understood at present.

Placodont Anatomy

Because placodonts were adapted for living in shallow near-shore ocean environments, their anatomy was optimized to help them plod along the seafloor looking for stationary prey such as hard-shelled mollusks and crustaceans.

Placodonts fall into two body types: the unarmored placodonts, informally known as the Placodontoidea, and the armored placodonts, known as the Cyamodontoidea. Body characteristics of the placodonts included:

Skull. The placodont skull was strong and heavily built. It was flat and wide in shape.

Sturdy jaws and crushing teeth. Placodonts ate very hard-shelled animals. Their ability to seize and crush these creatures with their jaws was the key to their survival. For grabbing, they had peglike, forward-pointing teeth at the front of their jaws and short, rounded teeth on the sides. For crushing, they had flat, tilelike tooth surfaces in the back of their mouths. Massive jaw muscles helped the placodont crush a mollusk's protective shell like a nut in a nut-cracker. Once the shell had been pulverized, the placodont could eat the soft body of the mollusk hiding inside. The front teeth were weaker or absent in the armored placodonts, being replaced in at least one kind—*Henodus* ("one tooth")—by a toothless beak similar to that of a turtle.

Backbone. The backbone of the placodonts was thick and strong. The short neck and tail were flexible but the back portion was locked firmly together, making the trunk of the animal inflexible. This suggests that the placodont's only means of propelling itself through the water was by moving its short tail.

Short, stumpy legs. The legs of placodonts were similar to those of land-dwelling reptiles. The five fingers and toes on each limb may have been covered with webbing to give them a more paddlelike appearance, similar to the limbs of turtles. The legs were short and could be used to help the animal move through the water, but not with great speed. As above, the tail was probably a placodont's primary means of propulsion. The feet could have been used to steer and guide it over the sea floor.

Body shape. The unarmored placodonts had tall, long, rounded bodies. The armored placodonts were short and much flatter.

External armor. The Placodontoidea, or unarmored placodonts, had only a hint of external body armor in the form of a bony knob on top of each vertebral spine. In contrast, the Cyamodontoidea, or armored placodonts, developed a broad, turtlelike shell on their backs (the carapace) as well as (in some kinds) armor on the neck, skull, and tail. Some cyamodontoids also had an armor-plated underside similar to the plastron seen in turtles.

Belly ribs. The unarmored placodonts, especially *Placodus*, had a belly reinforced by extensive belly ribs. Belly ribs are common to reptiles, but in the case of *Placodus,* they were highly developed. They not only strengthened the belly of the animal but angled upward to protect its sides as well. This cage of bones would have provided protection from predators but also provided support for the body when the animal walked on land.

Unlike some other marine reptiles that were highly adapted for ocean life, placodonts appear to have been able to crawl back on land when they wanted. In this way, their lives may have been similar to that of a turtle that can walk on land as well as swim in the water. It is conceivable that placodonts spent much of their time out of the water, perhaps (for example) to lay eggs during the breeding season. While this would have allowed them to avoid larger marine predators such as ichthyosaurs and nothosaurs, the land was not without its dangers. In either case, the unarmored placodonts in particular were probably easy prey. They were a distinct kind of marine reptile, caught in an existence that was neither totally aquatic nor totally terrestrial.

NOTHOSAURS, PLESIOSAURS, AND PLIOSAURS

The group of marine reptiles known as the Plesiosauria dominated the oceans of the Mesozoic for about 140 million years, up until the last days of the dinosaurs. Nested within the Plesiosauria were the subgroups Plesiosauroidea, the long-necked plesiosaurs, and the Pliosauroidea, the short-necked plesiosaurs. The Nothosauria, also discussed here, were a sister group of long-necked marine reptiles that evolved before the plesiosaurs. It is interesting to note, however, that at just about the time that the nothosaurs became extinct, at the end of the Late Triassic Epoch, the plesiosaurs were on the rise. It is likely that the plesiosaurs knocked the nothosaurs out of their ecological niches, taking over their role as a chief predator of the oceans.

Although they were not as fishlike as the ichthyosaurs, plesiosaurs and pliosaurs were adapted remarkably well for swimming. This can be seen in the design of their large, long paddles. The paddles were shaped like airplane wings: The front edge was thick and rounded and then tapered back to a narrower rear edge. They had evolved extra finger and toe bones to make the paddles longer. The parts of the shoulder and hip bones to which the paddles were attached were enormous compared with those of land-dwelling reptiles. This provided more surface area for the attachment of the huge muscles needed to propel these creatures through the water. The winglike shape of their paddles, combined with extensions of their unique shoulders and hips, made it possible for the Plesiosauria to "fly" underwater. They actually moved their paddles in graceful vertical strokes very much like the flapping wings of a bird in flight. A similar kind of swimming technique is seen in sea turtles, sea lions, and penguins today. Having two sets of "wings"—the front and rear paddles—gave plesiosaurs and pliosaurs power, speed, and maneuverability.

Nothosaurs are known only from the Triassic Period. Their fossils are almost exclusively limited to ancient ocean deposits in Europe, although a few remains have been found in China and Israel. Plesiosaurs and pliosaurs existed from the Late Triassic to the Late Cretaceous, and their remains are distributed on many continents, including Europe, North America, South America, Africa, Australia, and Antarctica.

Nothosaurus

Nothosaur Anatomy

Nothosaurs represent an early attempt of land-dwelling reptiles to find a home in the sea. Except for their webbed feet and long, streamlined necks, the earliest nothosaurs resemble lizards that simply took to the water to find food. Although the last of the nothosaurs had evolved paddles that made them better swimmers, they still moved about in the water by undulating their bodies from side to side. Their tail was the main source of their propulsion. Their shoulder and hip bones never changed in the way that they did in the plesiosaurs, which allowed plesiosaurs to adapt an underwater form of locomotion similar to flying. The lifestyle of nothosaurs was probably similar to that of today's sea lions. They sunned themselves on the shore and went into the ocean in search of fish when they were hungry. Nothosaurs probably laid their eggs on land like their fully terrestrial reptilian ancestors. Interestingly, specimens of the nothosaurlike sauropterygian *Keichousaurus* have recently been found with unborn young inside, indicating that these creatures (and possibly also nothosaurs) gave birth to live young.

Characteristics of the nothosaur body included:

Small to medium length. Most species of nothosaurs were only about 3 feet (1 m) long, although several larger kinds existed that measured about 10 to 13 feet (3 to 4 m). On average, the nothosaurs were much smaller than the plesiosaurs.

Long necks, tails, and bodies. The necks and tails of the nothosaurs were often about the same length, as in *Nothosaurus* and *Ceresiosaurus* ("Lake Lugano lizard").

Long, narrow snout and jaws. The front of the nothosaur snout was somewhat broad and spoon-shaped. The jaws were filled with long, curved, widely spaced needlelike teeth. The teeth interlocked when the jaws were closed, making them excellent tools for clamping down on fish.

Webbed feet. The feet of nothosaurs had five digits each. The feet of early nothosaurs such as *Nothosaurus* and *Lariosaurus* ("Lake Como lizard") were webbed, but still very lizardlike. Later nothosaurs, including *Ceresiosaurus*, developed longer toes and more paddlelike feet.

Flexible spine. One primary difference between the nothosaurs and plesiosaurs was in the spinal column. Nothosaurs swam by undulating their body rather than using their paddles like the plesiosaurs. The tail was the main source of propulsion for swimming. Undulating the body to wave the tail required a flexible spine that could bend from side to side.

Strong forelegs. The front legs of nothosaurs were often larger and stronger than the hind legs. This suggests that the front legs had a role in swimming, probably in making turns and supplementing the power provided by their tail.

Plesiosaur Anatomy

The Plesiosauria were more fully adapted to the ocean than the Nothosauria. It is difficult to imagine that they willfully crawled out of the water except when they were still young and small. Imagine how clumsy they would have been on land, dragging themselves along on their paddles. It would have made them extremely vulnerable to dinosaurs and other terrestrial predators. Even the sturdy belly ribs of a 30- to 50-foot (9 to 15 m) plesiosaur or pliosaur might not have been strong enough to support its enormous weight out of the water.

One plesiosaur from the Late Cretaceous was found with the remains of a pterosaur (flying reptile) in its stomach area along with a fish and a cephalopod still in its shell, swallowed whole. Another example found in 1998 provided even more evidence that plesiosaurs were adapted to eat hard-shelled creatures. The specimen from Japan had many remains of ammonite jaws left in its stomach area. The nautiluslike shells that once housed these creatures had evidently been dissolved by the digestive system of the plesiosaur.

Characteristics of the plesiosaur body included:

Medium to long length. Plesiosaurs ranged in length from about 12 to 46 feet (4 to 14 m). Most of this length, however, was taken up by the long neck and short tail. The body was proportionately small compared with the length of the neck.

Long necks, short tails. Unlike nothosaurs, in plesiosaurs, the neck was always much longer than the tail. The neck had from 29 to 72 vertebrae.

Broad but compact body. The plesiosaur body was stiff with an ellipsoid shape. The spine was not flexible, which provided further strength and leverage for the mighty paddles to do their work.

Strong ribs and belly ribs. The stiffness of the plesiosaur body was largely because of its numerous and heavily built ribs. These animals had strong, closely spaced ribs that extended down their sides as well as belly ribs that reinforced their underside. The belly ribs were so long that they almost met the ends of the side ribs, forming a stiff, bony cage for the body. The belly ribs were important for strengthening and protecting the body when the animal was in the water.

Small skull. The skull was broad and short, with a wide, flat snout with a pointed tip. It was triangular in shape when viewed from above.

Teeth and jaws. Plesiosaur teeth were long, sharp, and conical. They were embedded in bony sockets that lined the sides and front of the upper and lower jaws. These teeth were widely enough spaced so that they would interlock when the jaws clamped down on prey. The teeth sometimes pointed outwards from the jaw. Some plesiosaurs, such as *Dolichorhynchops* ("long snout face") and *Libonectes* ("southwest wind swimmer"), had long, caninelike fangs in the front part of the jaws. They could lance soft, fleshy prey or penetrate the hard shell of mollusks.

Long, wing-shaped paddles. The paddles of a plesiosaur were highly elongated because of the addition of bones to its fingers and toes. All four paddles were about the same length. They were wing-shaped and allowed the animal to move them up and down to "fly" underwater like a penguin. The ichthyosaurs were most certainly fast swimmers as well.

The long necks of the nothosaurs and plesiosauroids likely slowed them down. It would have been difficult for many long-necked plesiosauroids to pursue their prey in a high-speed chase. Just how the long neck affected plesiosauroid behavior is a matter of speculation. These animals could have hunted using an ambush style, waiting for fishes to pass and lashing out with their necks to snare a few with their wicked teeth. This makes sense for an animal with a long neck, because it could conceal its body behind a rock or other obstacle so that it was hidden from the view of approaching fish. Another view of plesiosaur hunting was proposed in 2006 by paleontologist Leslie Noe of the Sedgwick Museum in Cambridge, England. By modeling the neck of a long-necked plesiosaur, Noe determined that the interlocking vertebrae of the neck and back would have made it difficult for the animal to lift its head, rotate its neck, or move the neck from side to side. The most natural movement would have been a downward bend just below the body of the animal. Noe pictured the plesiosaur as a bottom feeder, picking up mollusks from the ocean floor as it hovered overhead. This hypothesis has been supported by the discovery of mollusk remains as presumed gut contents in the ribcages of some plesiosaur specimens.

Pliosaur Anatomy

With their large heads and streamlined bodies, pliosaurs were probably capable of quick movement and sustained chases at high speed. They were pursuit predators, but not as fast as ichthyosaurs. They would chase large prey until they could grab them in their powerful jaws. Pliosaur teeth were sturdy, cone-shaped, and sharp, capable of cutting through thick flesh and even bones. Their mouths were huge, making any sea creature of the time a possible meal, including the long-necked plesiosaurs, ichthyosaurs, and the largest fishes and mollusks of the time. Pliosaurs were the top predator of the oceans throughout much of the Mesozoic, filling a niche similar to that of the killer whale today.

The stomach contents of one specimen of a subadult *Liopleurodon* ("smooth-sided tooth") revealed that it ate fishes and belemnites—small squidlike creatures with a hard, conelike inner shell. Paleontologist Darren Naish has suggested that young pliosaurs may have subsisted on a diet of smaller prey such as small mollusks and fishes, trading up to large prey when they became adults. Evidence that a pliosaur once ate a dinosaur is slim, but tantalizing. It consists of armor plates from the hide of a dinosaur that were found within proximity of a pliosaur skeleton.

Characteristics of the pliosaur body included:

Long length. Pliosaurs were huge, up to 50 feet (15 m) long. They were the largest members of the Plesiosauria.

Huge skull. The skull was long and strong with a long, tapering snout. The head was shaped like an elongated triangle when viewed from above. The skulls of some pliosaurs were one-quarter their total body length. The largest skulls were more than 10 feet (3 m) long.

Short necks, short tails. The necks of pliosaurs were short when compared to those of plesiosaurs. They had from 17 to 26 neck vertebrae, with a tendency towards shorter necks in the later kinds of pliosaurs. Their tails were short.

Broad, long, streamlined body. Unlike the plesiosaurs—where the neck was long—the body of a pliosaur made up most of its length. Pliosaurs were streamlined, powerful swimmers. Nearing the end of the Mesozoic Era, their body shape had begun to approach that of the ichthyosaurs. This undoubtedly made them faster swimmers than their long-necked relatives, the plesiosaurs. The spine was rigid, providing strength and leverage for the paddles to swing up and down.

Strong ribs and belly ribs. Like plesiosaurs, pliosaurs had extensive side and belly ribs. This added stiffness to the body and may have allowed a pliosaur to crawl out of the water onto dry land without collapsing under its own weight, although this idea is disputed by some scientists today who think that these creatures were simply too heavy to leave the water.

Teeth and jaws. Pliosaur teeth were stout, sharp, and conical. They lined the sides and front of the upper and lower jaws and were widely spaced. The teeth in the front part of the jaws were longer than those in the rear. Some protruded outwards. Considering the large size of the prey that a pliosaur ate, the teeth were mainly used to grab and crush its victims with the brute force of its muscular jaws.

Long, wing-shaped paddles. The wing-shaped paddles of pliosaurs were highly elongated, as in plesiosaurs. Once difference between plesiosaur and pliosaur paddles was that in a pliosaur, the hind paddles were longer and stronger than the front paddles. This suggests a slightly different form of propulsion that relied more on the "flight" of the rear paddles than the front ones, perhaps because this animal was capable of swimming fast in pursuit of its prey.

THE MOSASAURS

Mosasaurs retain many of the attributes of their terrestrial ancestors. Unlike ichthyosaurs and plesiosaurs, which are presumed to have had smooth skin, mosasaurs still had reptilian scales. Their ancestry can be traced to ancient snakes, although for many years some paleontologists have thought that mosasaurs were more closely related to extinct monitor lizards. Mosasaur species ranged in size from the length of a minibus to that of the longest tractor-trailer, from about 10 to 57 feet (3 to 17.5 m).

Mosasaurs were the latecomers of the Mesozoic marine reptiles. They first appeared about 90 million years ago, during the Late Cretaceous. By that time, the ichthyosaurs were nearly extinct and the last act of the non-avian dinosaurs was being played out. One reason the mosasaurs were successful was that they probably helped fill the ecological niche left open by the demise of the fish- and squid-eating ichthyosaurs. Mosasaurs competed with many other formidable creatures in the ocean, particularly the remaining giants of the marine reptiles—the plesiosaurs and pliosaurs.

Mosasaurs radiated rapidly and spread across much of the globe. A few million years after they originated, they were already the most dominant type of marine reptile. During their Late Cretaceous reign, they spread to all the major oceans of the world, nearly from pole to pole. Their remains have been found in such widespread locations as the United States, Canada, Europe, South America, North Africa, the Middle East, New Zealand, and even Antarctica.

Mosasaur Anatomy

The sharp, conical teeth of mosasaurs were able to cut through or crush most any kind of fleshy or bony creature they could fit inside their mouth. Mosasaurs probably hunted by lying in wait and ambushing their prey. Some mosasaurs had a bony rod at the end of the snout, and it has been suggested that they used it to ram their prey, stunning them.

All mosasaurs shared the following anatomical traits:

Many sizes. The largest mosasaurs, including *Mosasaurus* and *Tylosaurus* ("knob [snout] lizard"), could exceed 50 feet (15 m) in length. The smallest, such as *Clidastes* ("one who locks" [referring to its vertebrae]) were often between 10 and 13 feet (3 and 4 m) long.

Skull. Mosasaur skulls were not overly huge in comparison with the rest of their bodies. They were tall and broad at the base and narrowed towards the snout. They had an extended triangular shape when viewed from above.

Teeth and jaws. Mosasaur teeth were pointed, conical, and slightly curved. The teeth were stout and strong but prone to break-ing. Being reptiles, mosasaurs would have continuously replaced their worn or lost teeth with new ones. The teeth were set into bony sockets and were widely spaced. One of the differences seen between kinds of mosasaurs was the size and position of the larger teeth that were in the front of the upper jaw. These caninelike fangs were sometimes much longer than the other teeth. Mosasaur jaws were strong. The animals were able to attack large prey that put up a fight. It appears that they often broke their teeth while biting into bones. One unusual kind of mosasaur—*Globidens* ("globular tooth")—had teeth unlike other mosasaurs. Its teeth were rounded instead of pointed, indicating that it may have been a shallow-water eater of mollusks, using its blunt teeth to crush the shells of its prey. Some mosasaurs—such as those in the clade Plioplatecarpinae—could expand their upper and lower jaws to eat large prey. A similar ability is also seen in snakes. A few oddball mosasaurs did not quite fit the mold of the others. *Pluridens* ("many teeth") from West Africa had greatly elongated jaws and a battery of stocky, slightly curved teeth similar to those found in early ich-thyosaurs. *Pluridens* had twice as many teeth as other mosasaurs and may have used its jaws to snare fish from the water or to crush thin-shelled cephalopods. Another kind, *Goronyosaurus* ("Goronyo lizard"), developed a head that was very crocodilelike, despite the fact that crocodiles and mosasaurs are not related. Unlike other mosasaurs but similar to living crocodiles, this creature apparently also moved away from the coastal waters of the ocean to inland lagoons.

Body and tail. The mosasaur body was narrow and long with a long, broad tail. The spine was flexible and the animal propelled itself by undulating its body from side to side like a swimming crocodile. The tail would have magnified this propulsion and helped steer the animal.

Short paddles. The hands and feet of mosasaurs had evolved into short, flesh-covered paddles. They had four or five digits per paddle and the front paddles were often longer than the rear paddles. Mosasaur paddles remained more like reptile feet and retained a kind of wrist or ankle that had been lost in plesiosaur feet. The paddles were used for changing direction and maneuvering.

Skin. The skin of mosasaurs was scaly, similar to that of modern snakes. In most cases, the scales were diamond-shaped and smooth, giving little resistance to the water while the animal swam. Some mosasaurs had a different form of scale, such as the bumpy scales of *Clidastes.*

A recent discovery showed that mosasaurs, like ichthyosaurs, gave birth to live young while in the water. This was seen in a specimen of *Plioplatecarpus* ("more *Platecarpus*") discovered in 1996. The remains of two unborn mosasaurs were found within the body cavity of the mother. Without any evidence of eggshells, it was possible to conclude that this was the first positive evidence that mosasaurs gave birth to live young. As in ichthyosaurs, the young probably left the birth canal tail first and then raced to the surface to get a gulp of air. After that, they were probably left on their own, and may have fled to shallow waters to find a place to hide from large predators.

EXTINCT MARINE CROCODILES

Today's crocodiles are what remain of a long line of reptiles that first appeared during the Middle Triassic Epoch. Only a few kinds survive today, including crocodiles, alligators, and gavials.

Forms of crocodiles that lived in the ocean were highly successful during the Jurassic and Cretaceous Periods. They returned to the sea, as did other forms of reptiles, to take advantage of abundant food supplies in the form of fishes, cephalopods, and other marine reptiles. Nearly all marine crocodiles were extinct by the end of the Mesozoic Era. The only living crocodile that is at all adapted for marine life is *Crocodylus porosus*, the Australian saltwater crocodile, which is not related to extinct marine crocodiles. It is most often found in shallow estuaries and coastal swamps rather than in the open ocean.

Fossils of marine crocodiles are found on many continents. They seemed to have found the most success in shallow saltwater environments, including the perimeter of what is called the **Tethys Ocean**—a shallow ocean that once covered much of Europe and North Africa, separating them from each other and Asia. Marine crocodiles were most successful during the Middle and Late Jurassic Epochs. Some forms were highly adapted to ocean life, while others retained much of the armor and leg design of their terrestrial ancestors.

Like all seagoing reptiles, marine crocodiles were air-breathing creatures that could grow and feed in saltwater oceans. The fossils of marine crocodiles are found only in deposits made in ocean environments.

Marine Crocodile Anatomy

Although the head was generally more lightly built with a long, narrow snout, extinct marine crocodiles resembled today's crocodiles in many ways. Here are some of the anatomical features that marine crocodiles share:

Long, narrow skull. The skulls of marine crocodiles were lightweight and had a long, narrow snout. When viewed from above, they had an extremely elongated triangular shape.

Eyes on the sides. The eyes of marine crocodiles were on the sides of the skull rather than the top as in most living crocodiles. This gave them a wider field of vision while underwater.

Jaws and teeth. The long jaws had closely spaced, pointed, cone-shaped teeth. These were for grabbing fish.

Tail and feet adapted for swimming. Marine crocodiles propelled themselves by waving their tails back and forth. This was aided by thrusts from the hind legs. The front legs were probably of little use during swimming and were probably held at the side. The crocodiles that were most highly adapted for ocean life were the metriorhyn-chids. They had replaced their webbed reptilian feet with paddles. The rear paddles were larger than the front paddles. In other marine crocodiles, the feet were webbed but had not evolved into paddles. The front limbs were often reduced in size so that they could be tucked back while the animal was swimming.

Loss of armor. Some marine crocodiles showed a reduction in body armor, especially on the back. Protective armor on the back was a holdover from their land-dwelling days and was unnecessary in the water. Losing armor would have also lightened the body and made it more streamlined for swimming. In the metriorhynchids, the body armor was nonexistent, replaced by a smooth skin. The other clades of marine crocodiles were much less advanced in this way. The dyrosaurids had only light armor on the back.

Streamlining of body and tail. The body of marine crocodiles was long and somewhat narrow when compared with that of their land-living relatives. The head and snout came to a narrow point. The tail was long and flattened vertically to offer less water resistance and to serve as a more effective paddle. In the metriorhynchids, the end of the tail had a vertical fin to provide additional thrust, a sign that these animals could probably dive deeply. One metriorhynchid, *Metriorhynchus* ("moderate snout"), even had small armor plates in front of the eyes to protect them and improve the smooth contour of the head for swimming.

Extinct marine crocodiles fell into four main groups, or clades. Of these, the members of the Metriorhynchidae were clearly best designed for ocean life. Metriorhynchids such as *Metriorhynchus* and *Geosaurus* ("Earth lizard") were probably capable of sustained outings in the ocean and deep diving. Other forms of marine crocodiles show indications that they were evolving ocean-going body features similar to those of the metriorhynchids. The clade that was least adapted for ocean life was the Pholidosauridae, a group dominated by freshwater crocodiles. At least one member of this clade, named *Terminonaris* ("end nose"), has been found in ocean deposits, however. Its thick tail and heavy back armor

Metriorhynchus

gave it an appearance that is much more like those of today's inland and freshwater crocodiles than those of typical marine crocodiles.

Marine crocodiles were probably similar to mosasaurs in their hunting and eating habits. They were probably not capable of long, sustained periods of high-speed swimming. This suggests that they were ambush predators, waiting for prey to come near and then thrusting out with their powerful bodies to snatch them. Unlike mosasaurs, marine crocodiles had lightly built, narrow jaws. This would have made them ill-equipped for doing battle with large creatures. Their teeth were short and pointed and best suited for grabbing fleshy prey such as fishes and squids.

It is assumed that marine crocodiles primarily ate fish. Some interesting stomach contents, however, have been discovered for one species of *Metriorhynchus*. A set of fossil remains from England show that the animal had eaten small, hard-shelled ammonites, squidlike belemnites, parts of a large fish, and even a pterosaur.

EXTINCT MARINE TURTLES

Another group of reptiles from the Mesozoic that survives to this day are the turtles. Their origins reach back before the Age of Dinosaurs, to the end of the Permian Period and the Early Triassic Epoch, more than 210 million years ago. The first forms of turtles were land animals.

Marine turtles first appeared in the Early Cretaceous Epoch. Along with mosasaurs, they were among the last group of the great marine reptiles to take to the oceans. All species of Mesozoic marine turtles are now extinct, although a number of their relatives, including the green turtle and leatherback turtle, survive today.

One group of ancient marine turtles stood out among them all. They were members of the group Protostegidae and included the largest marine turtles ever to swim the oceans. The largest of the protostegids was *Archelon*, a huge beast that measured 13 feet (4 m) in length. It is a good example of how the land-dwelling turtles adapted so that they could thrive in the ocean.

Marine Turtle Anatomy

Marine turtles evolved several features to improve their ability to live in the ocean. The most obvious changes were to develop a more lightweight, streamlined body that could propel itself in the water.

The shell of a turtle has two parts. The top part, protecting its back, is called the *carapace*. The bottom part, protecting its belly, is the *plastron*. The shells of land-dwelling turtles are designed to enclose the body in a tightly knit mosaic of bony plates. This was an effective form of protection against predators. A turtle adapted for the ocean needed to modify the heavy body armor to enable it to swim effectively. The great giant marine turtles of the Late Cretaceous evolved several modifications in their shell and body to make life in the ocean easier.

Archelon had a shell that was greatly reduced in mass. Instead of a solid carapace, it only had a light bony framework covered with skin. The plastron was also reduced and consisted only of bony coverings under the attachments of its four limbs. One of the most remarkable adaptations of *Archelon* for ocean life was its paddles. Instead of webbed feet like those of freshwater turtles, its fingers and toes had been greatly elongated and transformed into effective paddles. The front paddles were enormous and must have been its primary source of locomotion.

Other anatomical traits of extinct marine turtles included:

Large skull. The skulls of marine turtles were tall and long, with a pronounced beak at the tip of the snout. The jaws were probably weak. They may have used the beak and a hard surface inside the mouth for crushing softer crustaceans, but they were best suited for eating soft, floating creatures such as jellyfish. They did not have teeth.

Eyes on the sides. The eyes of marine turtles were on the side of the skull rather than the top, giving them a wide field of vision underwater or at the surface.

Feet adapted for swimming. Marine turtles had front and rear paddles instead of webbed feet. They pulled themselves along with their powerful front paddles. Their fingers and toes had become greatly elongated to make the paddles longer and wider. The front paddles were about twice the size of the rear ones.

Loss of armored shell. The carapace of marine turtles had been reduced to a set of lightweight, bony spokes. They were covered with skin to give the appearance of a complete carapace. The plastron was replaced with four smaller bony plates, each covering one of the limb attachments. These lightweight shells made swimming easier.

Streamlining of the body. Although it would be laughable to say that marine turtles were as streamlined as some of the other marine reptiles, the reduction of their bony armor certainly made for smoother sailing in the water. Their paddles and head also had smooth contours to cut through the water with ease. While these animals were not speed demons, they could probably swim with grace and control.

The members of the clade Protostegidae were the most highly adapted Mesozoic marine turtles. They lived during the time of mosasaurs, pliosaurs, marine crocodiles, and other formidable sea monsters. They must have had only limited success in competing with these other creatures for food, and were sometimes attacked by some of the larger predators of the time.

One specimen of *Archelon* was found without one of its limbs, presumably bitten off by a large predator. Without a well-armored shell, the only defense for these turtles was to try and make an escape.

Protostegids were probably not good deep-water divers, so they swam near the surface most of the time, skimming the upper waters for jellyfish and planktonic creatures such as small ammonites. They may have also lived in shallow coastal waters rather then risking the danger of the open ocean where other giant creatures could attack them.

Marine turtles were probably most vulnerable when they came ashore to lay eggs. There, they would have been subject to attack by large carnivorous dinosaurs and crocodiles. Newly hatched sea turtle babies would have been frequent victims of predatory flying reptiles, birds, and small dinosaurs.

SUMMARY

This chapter provided an overview of the major families of extinct marine reptiles that lived during the Mesozoic Era.

1. Marine reptiles were air-breathing creatures that lived in the water. Like today's turtles and crocodiles, they would hold their breath while under water.
2. Marine reptiles are grouped in the following categories: *ichthyosaurs*, tuna- or dolphinlike in appearance, but unrelated to them; *placodonts,* small to medium-sized, bottom-feeding reptiles that resembled armor-plated walruses; *nothosaurs*, streamlined, swift, seal-like predators; *plesiosaurs*, large long- and short-necked open-ocean predators; *marine crocodiles*, several kinds of ocean-going crocodiles; *mosasaurs*, swift predators with short necks and powerful jaws; and *marine turtles*, the first true seagoing turtles.

3. Marine reptiles adapted to ocean life by optimizing anatomical traits that reduced drag and provided them with speed and maneuverability in the water.

4. Features such as webbed or flipperlike limbs and a vertical flattening of the tail aided in locomotion and could have also helped them to dive deep.

5. The ichthyosaur *Shonisaurus* is now the largest of all known marine reptiles, measuring about 77 feet (23 m) long.

CONCLUSION

Extinction of the Dinosaurs

The last of the non-avian dinosaurs, primitive birds, pterosaurs, all marine reptiles except turtles, and ammonites became extinct about 65.5 million years ago, at a point in time that geologists call the **K-T extinction**. The name of the extinction signifies a division in time between the Cretaceous (*kreta* in Latin) and Tertiary, or Neogene, Periods. The K-T event was a mass extinction, wiping out at least 50 percent of all animal life alive at the time. Even those groups of organisms that survived, including plants, insects, other invertebrates, fishes, frogs, salamanders, turtles, lizards, crocodiles, birds, and mammals, lost great numbers of species. Extinction is a natural occurrence: the irreversible elimination of an entire species of organism. Once it occurs, there is no turning back. It is happening all of the time. More than 99.9 percent of all the species of organisms that have ever lived are now extinct.

Chief among the causes of extinction are environmental changes that affect the food supply or body chemistry of organisms, disease, and natural disasters (such as volcanic eruptions, earthquakes, and the changing surface of the Earth).

Evidence has been mounting that the great K-T extinction was caused by the collision of a large asteroid with the Earth. Debris thrown into the atmosphere from such a collision could have blackened the skies and poisoned the air for many months, maybe even years. If the poisoning affected oceanic ecosystems, it might have led to the demise of the mosasaurs and other remaining marine reptiles. Plankton forms the base of most oceanic food chains, and

The extinction of the dinosaurs possibly was capped by the collision of Earth with a giant asteroid.

we know that much of it was wiped-out by the K-T extinction event. Many of the creatures that predatory marine reptiles would have fed upon were probably plankton eaters. So, the demise of plankton would have led to demise of plankton eaters, and eventually marine reptiles would have nothing left to eat but themselves.

The K-T extinction brought an end to the great era of reptiles and ushered in a new age during which mammals would soon rise to dominate environments all over the Earth. The great clades of marine reptiles arose and diminished during different times of the Mesozoic. Several of them, such as ichthyosaurs, had already come and gone by the end of the Cretaceous Period.

The Rise of Mammals will explore the rapid diversification and radiation of the mammals following the extinction of the non-avian dinosaurs.

GEOLOGIC TIME SCALE

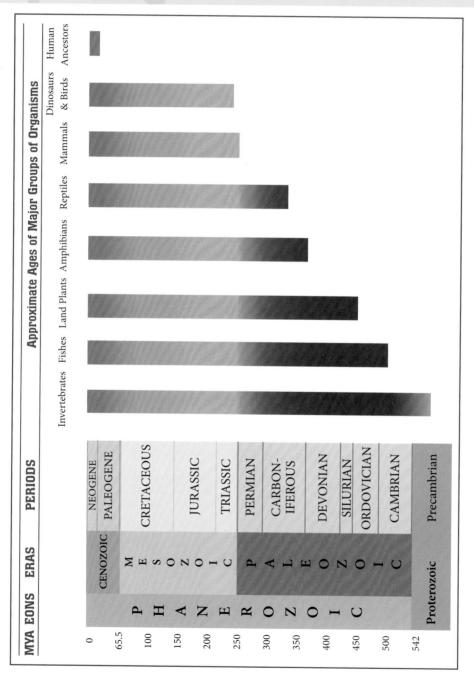

Appendix Two: Positional Terms

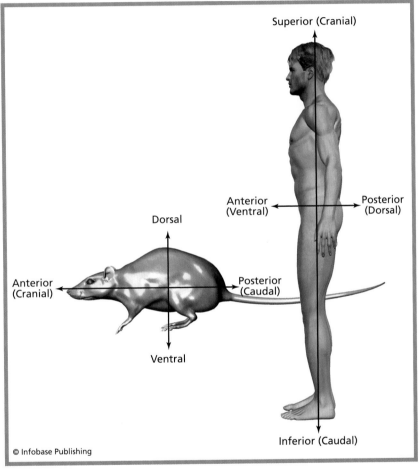

Superior (Cranial)

Anterior (Ventral)

Posterior (Dorsal)

Dorsal

Anterior (Cranial)

Posterior (Caudal)

Ventral

Inferior (Caudal)

© Infobase Publishing

Positional terms used to describe vertebrate anatomy

GLOSSARY

adaptations Anatomical, physiological, and behavioral changes that occur in an organism that enable it to survive environmental changes.

anatomy The basic biological systems of an animal, such as the skeletal and muscular systems.

angiosperms The flowering plants; plants utilizing flowers to attract pollinators, such as insects, and which also encase their seeds in fruits that can be dispersed separately from the plant.

anterior Directional term meaning toward the head, or cranial, end of a vertebrate.

arboreal Living in trees.

Archosauria The branch of diapsid reptiles including dinosaurs, pterosaurs, crocodiles, birds and kin.

articulated The condition of a fossil skeleton found with its bones in place, connected as they would have been in life.

Avialae A subclade of Dinosauria that includes all extinct and extant birds.

basal At the base or earliest level of evolutionary development; usually used when referring to an ancestral taxon.

binocular Involving two eyes.

bone bed Fossil locality with a high concentration of bones from more than one individual.

carnivorous Meat-eating.

clade A group of related organisms including all the descendants of a single common ancestor.

cladistic analysis An analytical technique for comparing the genetic, morphological, and behavioral traits of taxa.

climate The kind of weather that occurs at a particular place over time.

clutch A group of eggs in a nest.

coevolution A change, through natural selection, in the genetic makeup of one species in response to a genetic change in another.

continental drift   The slow and gradual movement and transformation of the continents because of shifting of the tectonic plates of Earth's crust.

convergent evolution   Term used to describe a situation in which unrelated species each develop similar adaptations to similar environmental conditions.

derived   Term used to describe a trait of an organism that is a departure from the most basal (ancestral) form.

diagnostic trait   A measurable feature in the morphology of a fossil that can be used to identify members of a given clade or taxon of extinct animal.

Diapsida   Amniotes with two temporal fenestrae: a lower one like the one seen in synapsids and a second one on top of the skull and behind the orbit.

dinosaur   Member of a clade of extinct ornithodiran archosaurian reptiles with an upright posture and either a saurischian or ornithischian style of hip.

ectothermic   Term used to describe a "cold-blooded" vertebrate.

endothermic   Term used to describe a "warm-blooded" vertebrate.

era   A span of geologic time ranking below the eon; the Archean Eon is divided into four eras dating from more than 4 billion years ago to 2.5 billion years ago; the Proterozoic Eon is divided into three eras dating from 2.5 billion years ago to about 542 million years ago; the Phanerozoic Eon is divided into three eras—the Paleozoic, the Mesozoic, and the Cenozoic. The Paleozoic ("ancient life") Era lasted from 542 million to 251 million years ago; the Mesozoic ("middle life") Era lasted from 251 million to 65.5 million years ago; the Cenozoic ("recent life") Era began 65 million years ago and continues to the present.

evolution   The natural process by which species gradually change over time, controlled by changes to the genetic code—the DNA—of organisms and whether or not those changes enable an organism to survive in a given environment.

extant   Term used to describe an organism that is living today; not extinct.

extinction   The irreversible elimination of an entire species of organism because it cannot adapt effectively to changes in its environment.

fauna   Animals found in a given ecosystem.

femur   Upper leg bone.

fenestrae   Openings or "windows" in the vertebrate skull, just behind the orbit on the side of the skull, or temple region.

flora   Plants found in a given ecosystem.

forelimbs   The two front legs of a vertebrate.

fossil   Any physical trace or remains of prehistoric life.

gastroliths   Stones swallowed by an animal, often to aid in the crushing and processing of food once it has been swallowed.

genus   (plural: genera) A taxonomic name for one or more closely related organisms that is divided into species; names of organisms, such as *Tyrannosaurus rex*, are composed of two parts: the genus name (first) and the species name (second).

Gondwana   Name given to Earth's southern landmass during the Mesozoic Era; formed by the breakup of Pangaea, Gondwana included regions that would become the continents of South America, Africa, India, Australia, and Antarctica.

gymnosperms   Seed plants, such as conifers, that have a protective cone or other body for their seed embryos.

herbivore   An animal whose primary food source is vegetation.

hind limbs   The two rear legs of a vertebrate.

K-T extinction   Mass extinction of the dinosaurs and other organisms that occurred at the boundary between the Late Cretaceous Epoch and the Tertiary (Paleogene) Period.

Laurasia   Name given to Earth's northern landmass during the Mesozoic Era; formed by the breakup of Pangaea, Laurasia included regions that would become the continents of North America, Europe, and Asia.

mass extinction   An extinction event that kills off more than 25 percent of all species in a million years or less.

maxilla   Major tooth-bearing bone of the upper jaw.

metabolism   The combination of all biochemical processes that take place in an organism to keep it alive.

monophyletic   A natural clade of animals descended from a common ancestor.

morphological   Pertaining to the body form and structure of an organism.

natural selection   One of Darwin's observations regarding the way in which evolution works; given the complex and changing conditions under which life exists, those individuals with the combination of inherited traits best suited to a particular environment wil survive and reproduce while others will not.

neural spine   A bony, upward-pointing process on a vertebra, the function of which was muscle attachment.

non-avian   A nonflying animal; term used to distinguish non-avian dinosaurs from birds.

omnivorous   Term used to describe an animal with a diet consisting of plants and meat.

optic   Related to the sense of vision.

Ornithischia   One of the two clades of dinosaurs; characterized by a "bird-hipped" pelvis.

paleontologist   A scientist who studies prehistoric life, usually using fossils.

period   A span of geologic time ranking below the era; the Phanerozoic Eon is divided into three eras and 11 periods, each covering a span of millions of years; the longest of these periods, including the three in the Mesozoic Era, are further broken down into smaller divisions of time (epochs).

phylogeny   The family tree of a group of related organisms, based on evolutionary history.

physiology   The way in which an animal's parts work together and are adapted to help the organism survive.

population   Members of the same species that live in a particular area.

postcranial   "Behind the head"; term generally used to refer to the portion of the vertebrate skeleton other than the head.

posterior   Directional term meaning toward the tail end; also known as the caudal end.

predator   An animal that actively seeks, kills, and feeds on other animals.

premaxilla   The forward-most, often tooth-bearing portion of the upper jaw of most vertebrates.

pubis   Hip bone located below and in front of the acetabulum.

pygostyle   In birds, the pygostyle is part of the tail vertebrae and is a place of attachment for the tail feathers.

sacral vertebrae   Vertebrae that are fused to the pelvis.

sacrum   A vertebral unit consisting of several, often fused, vertebrae that supports an ilium on each side.

Saurischia   One of two clades of dinosaurs; characterized by a "lizard-hipped" pelvis.

Sauropoda   (Sauropods) Clade of long-necked, usually large, herbivorous dinosaurs.

Sauropodomorpha   Clade of archosaurs that includes "prosauropod" and sauropod dinosaurs.

sedimentary   Term used to describe rock that forms in layers from the debris of other rocks or the remains of organisms; sedimentary rock may contain fossils.

sexual dimorphism   Variation in morphology between the males and females of a species.

species   In classification, the most basic biological unit of living organisms; members of a species can interbreed and produce fertile offspring.

Synapsida   Amniotes with one temporal fenestra positioned somewhat behind and below the orbit.

taxa   (singular: taxon) In classification, a taxon is a group of related organisms, such as a clade, genus, or species.

Tethys Ocean   The ocean that bounded Pangaea on the east.

Theropoda   Clade of archosaurs including all carnivorous, and some secondarily herbivorous, dinosaurs.

tibia   Lowermost lower leg bone.

topography   Geologic character (elevation differences) of Earth's crust.

trackway   Series of sequential animal footprints.

transitional   Representing one step in the many stages that exist as species evolve.

vicariance biogeography   A theory stating that organisms are distributed geographically by riding on the backs of moving continents.

CHAPTER BIBLIOGRAPHY

Preface

Wilford, John Noble. "When No One Read, Who Started to Write?" *New York Times* (April, 6, 1999). Available online. URL: http://query. nytimes.com/gst/fullpage.html?res=9B01EFD61139F935A35757C0A9 6F958260. Accessed October 22, 2007.

Chapter 1 – The Early and Late Cretaceous Epochs

Berner, Robert A. "Atmospheric Oxygen Over Phanerozoic Time." *Proceedings of the National Academy of Sciences of the United States of America* 96, no. 20 (September 28, 1999): 10955–10957.

Chumakov, N.M. "Trends in Global Climate Changes Inferred from Geological Data." *Stratigraphy and Geological Correlation* 12, no. 2 (2004): 7–32.

Clemens, W.A., and L.G. Nelms. "Paleoecological Implications of Alaskan Terrestrial Vertebrate Fauna in Latest Cretaceous Time at High Paleolatitudes." *Geology* 21 (1993): 503–506.

Constantine, A., A. Chinsamy, P. Vickers-Rich, and T.H. Rich. "Periglacial Environments and Polar Dinosaurs." *South African Journal of Science* 94 (1998): 137–141.

Ellis, Richard. *No Turning Back: The Life and Death of Animal Species.* New York: Harper Collins, 2004.

Fiorillo, A.R., and R.A. Gangloff. "The Caribou Migration Model for Arctic Hadrosaurs (Dinosauria: Ornithischia): A Reassessment." *Historical Biology* 15 (2001): 323–334.

Kious, W. Jacquelyne, and Robert I. Tilling. *This Dynamic Earth: The Story of Plate Tectonics.* Washington, D.C.: United States Geological Survey, 2001.

Morgans, Helen S., and Stephen P. Hesselbo. "The Seasonal Climate of the Early-Middle Jurassic, Cleveland Basin, England." *Palaios* 14 (1999): 261–272.

Palmer, Douglas. *Atlas of the Prehistoric World.* New York: Discovery Books, 1999.

Pasch, A.D., and K.C. May. "Taphonomy and Paleoenvironment of a Hadrosaur (Dinosauria) from the Matanuska Formation (Turonian) in South-Central Alaska." In *Mesozoic Vertebrate Life*, edited by D.H. Tanke and K. Carpenter, 219–236. Bloomington: Indiana University Press, 2001.

Raup, David M. *Extinction: Bad Genes or Bad Luck?* New York: W.W. Norton, 1991.

Rees, Peter M., Alfred M. Ziegler, and Paul J. Valdes. *Jurassic Phytogeography and Climates: New Data and Model Comparisons.* Cambridge: Cambridge University Press, 2000.

Rees, Peter M., Christopher R. Noto, J. Michael Parrish, and Judith T. Parrish. "Late Jurassic Climates, Vegetation, and Dinosaur Distributions." *Journal of Geology* 112 (2004): 643–653.

Ross, Charles A., George T. Moore, and Darryl N. Hayashida. "Late Jurassic Paleoclimate Simulation—Paleoecological Implications for Ammonoid Provinciality." *Palaios* 7 (1992): 487–507.

Saltzman, Barry. *Dynamical Paleoclimatology: Generalized Theory of Global Climate Change.* New York: Academic Press, 2002.

Stevens, K.A., and J.M. Parrish. "Digital Reconstructions of Sauropod Dinosaurs and Implications for Feeding." In *The Sauropods: Evolution and Paleobiology,* edited by J.A. Wilson and K. Curry Rogers, 178–200. Berkeley: University of California Press, 2005.

———. "Neck Posture and Feeding Habits of Two Jurassic Sauropod Dinosaurs." *Science* 284 (1999): 798–800.

Chapter 2 – The Sauropods Diversify

Bakker, Robert T. *The Dinosaur Heresies.* New York: William Morrow, 1986.

———. "Ecology of the Brontosaurs." *Nature* 229 (January 15, 1971): 172–174.

Benton, Michael J. *Vertebrate Paleontology,* 3rd ed. Oxford: Blackwell Publishing, 2005.

Bonnan, Matthew F. "The Evolution of Manus Shape in Sauropod Dinosaurs: Implications for Functional Morphology, Forelimb Orientation, and Phylogeny." *Journal of Vertebrate Paleontology* 23, no. 3 (September 2003): 595–613.

———. "Morphometric Analysis of Humerus and Femur Shape in Morrison Sauropods: Implications for Functional Morphology and Paleobiology." *Paleobiology* 30, no. 3 (2004): 444–470.

———. "Pes Anatomy in Sauropod Dinosaurs: Implications for Functional Morphology, Evolution, and Phylogeny." In *Thunder-Lizards: The Sauropodomorph Dinosaurs,* edited by K. Carpenter and V. Tidwell, 346–380. Bloomington: Indiana University Press, 2005.

———. "The Evolution and Functional Morphology of Sauropod Dinosaur Locomotion." Ph.D. dissertation, Northern Illinois University (2001).

Bonnan, Matthew F., and Mathew J. Wedel. "First Occurrence of *Brachiosaurus* (Dinosauria: Sauropoda) from the Upper Jurassic Morrison Formation of Oklahoma." *PaleoBios* 24, no. 2 (September 15, 2004): 13–21.

Carpenter, Kenneth, Karl F. Hirsch, and John R. Horner, eds. *Dinosaur Eggs and Babies.* Cambridge: Cambridge University Press, 1994.

Carpenter, Kenneth. *Eggs, Nests, and Baby Dinosaurs: A New Look at Dinosaur Reproduction.* Bloomington: Indiana University Press, 1999.

Chiappe, Luis M., Rodolfo A. Coria, Lowell Dingus, Frankie Jackson, Anusuya Chinsamy, and Marilyn Fox. "Sauropod Dinosaur Embryos from the Late Cretaceous of Patagonia." *Nature* 396 (November 19, 1998): 258–261.

Clarke, Tom. "Dinosaur Faces Rearranged." News@Nature.com. Available online. URL: http://www.nature.com/news/2001/010809/full/news010809-2.html. Accessed March 24, 2008.

Colbert, Edwin H. *The Great Dinosaur Hunters and Their Discoveries.* New York: Dover Publications, 1984.

Colbert, Edwin H., Raymond B. Cowles, and Charles M. Bogert. "Rates of Temperature Increase in the Dinosaurs." *Copeia* 1947, no. 2 (June 30, 1947): 141–142.

Currie, Philip J., and Kevin Padian, eds. *Encyclopedia of Dinosaurs.* New York: Academic Press, 1997.

Fastovsky, David E., and David B. Weishampel. *The Evolution and Extinction of the Dinosaurs*, 2nd ed. Cambridge: Cambridge University Press, 2005.

Gillooly, James F., Andrew P. Allen, and Eric L. Charnov. "Dinosaur Fossils Predict Body Temperatures." *PloS Biology* 4, no. 8 (August 2006).

Hohnke, Lyle A., "Haemodynamics in the Sauropoda." *Nature* 244 (August 3, 1973): 309–310.

Hopkin, Michael. "Tiny Dino Discovered." News@Nature.com. Available online. URL: http://www.nature.com/news/2006/060605/full/news060605-8.html Accessed March 24, 2008.

Kennedy, Elaine. "Dinosaur Gastroliths or 'Gastromyths'?" *Geoscience Reports* 35 (2003): 1–4.

Ksepka, Daniel T., and Mark A. Norell. "*Erketu ellisoni*, a Long-Necked Sauropod from Bor Guvé (Dornogov Aimag, Mongolia)." *American Museum Novitates* 3508 (2006).

Lucas, Spencer G., Matthew C. Herne, Andrew B. Heckert, Adrian P. Hunt, and Robert M. Sullivan. "Reappraisal of *Seismosaurus*, a Late Jurassic Sauropod Dinosaur from New Mexico." *Proceedings*, Annual Meeting of the Society of Vertebrate Paleontology, November 7–10, 2004.

Norman, David. *Prehistoric Life: The Rise of the Vertebrates.* New York: Macmillan, 1994.

Pang, Qiqing, and Zhengwu Cheng. "A New Family of Sauropod Dinosaur from the Upper Cretaceous of Tianzhen, Shanxi Province, China." *Acta Geologica Sinica (English Edition)* 74, no. 2 (2000): 117–125.

Rauhut, Oliver W.M., Kristian Remes, Regina Fechner, Gerardo Cladera, and Pablo Puerta. "Discovery of a Short-Necked Sauropod Dinosaur from the Late Jurassic Period of Patagonia." *Nature* 435, no. 2 (June 2005): 670–672.

Rogers, Kristina C., and Catherine A. Forster. "The Last of the Dinosaur Titans: a New Sauropod from Madagascar." *Nature* 412 (August 2, 2001): 530–533.

Seymour, Roger S. "Dinosaurs, Endothermy and Blood Pressure." *Nature* 262 (July 15, 1976): 207–208.

Smith, Joshua B., Matthew C. Lamanna, Kenneth J. Lacovara, Peter Dodson, Jennifer R. Smith, Jason C. Poole, Robert Giegengack, and Yousry Attia. "A Giant Sauropod Dinosaur from an Upper Cretaceous Mangrove Deposit in Egypt." *Science* 292, no. 5522 (June 1, 2001): 1704–1706.

Stevens, Kent A., and J. Michael Parrish. "Neck Posture and Feeding Habits of Two Jurassic Sauropod Dinosaurs." *Science* 30, no. 284 (April 1999): 798–800.

———. "Neck Posture of Sauropod Dinosaurs." *Science* 30, no. 287 (January 28, 2000): 547b–547c.

Taylor, Michael P., and Darren Naish. "The Phylogenetic Taxonomy of Diplodocoidea (Dinosauria: Sauropoda)." *PaleoBios* 25, no. 2 (September 15, 2005): 1–7.

Upchurch, Paul, and John Martin. "The Anatomy and Taxonomy of *Cetiosaurus* (Saurischia, Sauropoda) from the Middle Jurassic of England." *Journal of Vertebrate Paleontology* 23, no. 1 (March 2003): 208–231.

Upchurch, Paul. "Neck Posture of Sauropod Dinosaurs." *Science* 30, no. 287 (January 28, 2000): 547b.

Wedel, Mathew J. "The Evolution of Vertebral Pneumaticity in Sauropod Dinosaurs." *Journal of Vertebrate Paleontology* 23, no. 2 (June 2003): 344–357.

———. "Vertebral Pneumaticity, Air Sacs, and the Physiology of Sauropod Dinosaurs." *Paleobiology* 29, no. 2 (June 2003): 243–255.

Wedel, Mathew J., Richard L. Cifelli, and R. Kent Sanders. "*Sauroposeidon proteles*, a New Sauropod from the Early Cretaceous of Oklahoma." *Journal of Vertebrate Paleontology* 20, no. 1 (2000): 109–114.

Weishampel, David B., Peter Dodson, and Halszka Osmólska, eds. *The Dinosauria*, 2nd ed. Berkeley: University of California Press, 2004.

Wilson, Jeffrey A. "Redescription of the Mongolian Sauropod *Nemegtosaurus mongoliensis* Nowinski (Dinosauria: Saurischia) and Comments on Late Cretaceous Sauropod Diversity." *Journal of Systematic Palaeontology* 3, no. 3 (August 24, 2005): 283–318.

———. "Sauropod Dinosaur Phylogeny: Critique and Cladistic Analysis." *Zoological Journal of the Linnaean Society* 136, no. 2 (October 2002): 217–276.

Chapter 3 – Theropod Giants and Feathered Dinosaurs

Abler, William L. "The Teeth of Tyrannosaurs." *Scientific American* (September 1999): 50–51.

———. "The Serrated Teeth of Tyrannosaurid Dinosaurs, and Biting Structure in Other Animals." *Paleobiology* 18, no. 2 (1992): 161–183.

Bakker, Robert T. *The Dinosaur Heresies*. New York: William Morrow, 1986.

Bakker, Robert T., and Peter M. Galton. "Dinosaur Monophyly and a New Class of Vertebrates." *Nature* 248 (March 8, 1974): 168–172.

Benton, Michael. *Vertebrate Paleontology*, 3rd ed. Oxford: Blackwell Publishing, 2005.

Buffetaut, Eric, Varavudh Suteethorn, and Haiyan Tong. "The Earliest Known Tyrannosaur from the Lower Cretaceous of Thailand." *Nature* 381 (June 20, 1996): 689–691.

Carpenter, Kenneth. "Variation in *Tyrannosaurus rex*." In *Dinosaur Systematics,* edited by Kenneth Carpenter and Philip J. Currie. Cambridge: Cambridge University Press, 1990.

Chatterjee, S., and R.J. Templin. "Biplane Wing Planform and Flight Performance of the Feathered Dinosaur *Microraptor gui*." *Proceedings of the National Academy of Sciences* 104 (2007): 1576–1580.

Currie, Philip J., and Kevin Padian, eds. *Encyclopedia of Dinosaurs*. New York: Academic Press, 1997.

Czerkas, S.A., and C. Yuan. "An Arboreal Maniraptoran from Northeast China." In *Feathered Dinosaurs and the Origin of Flight*, edited by S.J. Czerkas, 63–95. Blanding, Utah: The Dinosaur Museum, 2002.

Farlow, James O., and Michael K. Brett-Surman, eds. *The Complete Dinosaur*. Bloomington: Indiana University Press, 1999.

Farlow, James O., and Thomas R. Holtz Jr. "The Fossil Record of Predation in Dinosaurs." *Paleontological Society Papers* 8 (2002).

Farlow, James O., Stephen M. Gatesy, Thomas R. Holtz Jr., John R. Hutchinson, and John M. Robinson. "Theropod Locomotion." *American Zoologist* 40 (2000): 640–663.

Fastovsky, David E., and David B. Weishampel. *The Evolution and Extinction of the Dinosaurs*, 2nd ed. Cambridge: Cambridge University Press, 2005.

Franzosa, Jonathan W. "Evolution of the Brain in Theropoda (Dinosauria)." Ph.D. dissertation, The University of Texas at Austin (2004).

Gauthier, Jacques, and Kevin de Quieroz. "Feathered Dinosaurs, Flying Dinosaurs, Crown Dinosaurs, and the Name 'Aves.'" *New Perspectives on the Origin and Early Evolution of Birds*. New Haven: Peabody Museum of Natural History, Yale University (2001): 7–41.

Holtz, Thomas R. Jr. "A New Phylogeny of the Carnivorous Dinosaurs." *Gaia* 15 (December 1998): 5–61.

Hutchinson, John R., and Mariano Garcia. "*Tyrannosaurus* Was Not a Fast Runner." *Nature* 415 (February 28, 2002): 1018–1022.

Ji, Q., Z.-X. Luo, C.-X. Yuan, and A.R. Tabrum. "A Swimming Mammaliaform from the Middle Jurassic and Ecomorphological Diversification of Early Mammals." *Science* 311 (2006): 1123–1127.

Longrich, N. "Structure and function of hindlimb feathers in *Archaeopteryx lithographica*." *Paleobiology* 32 (2006): 417–431.

Lucas, Spencer G. *Dinosaurs: The Textbook*, 4th ed. New York: McGraw-Hill, 2004.

Norman, David. *Prehistoric Life: The Rise of the Vertebrates*. New York: Macmillan, 1994.

Rayfield, Emily J. "Aspects of Comparative Cranial Mechanics in the Theropod Dinosaurs *Coelophysis, Allosaurus* and *Tyrannosaurus.*" *Zoological Journal of the Linnaean Society* 144, no. 3 (July 2005): 309–316.

———. "Cranial Design and Function in a Large Theropod Dinosaur." *Nature* 409 (February 22, 2001): 1033–1037.

Sanders, R. Kent, and David K. Smith. "The Endocranium of the Theropod Dinosaur *Ceratosaurus* Studied with Computer Tomography." *Acta Palaeontologica Polonica* 50, no. 3 (2005): 601–616.

Stevens, Kent A. "Binocular Vision in Theropod Dinosaurs." *Journal of Vertebrate Paleontology* 26, no. 2 (June 2006): 321–330.

Weishampel, David B., Peter Dodson, and Halszka Osmólska, eds. *The Dinosauria*, 2nd ed. Berkeley: University of California Press, 2004.

Xu, X., and F. Zhang. "A New Maniraptoran Dinosaur from China with Long Feathers on the Metatarsus." *Naturwissenschaften* 92 (2005): 173–177.

Xu, X., Z. Zhou, X. Wang, X. Kuang, and X. Du. "Four-winged Dinosaurs from China." *Nature* 421 (2003): 335–340.

Xu, Xing, James M. Clark, Catherine A. Forster, Mark A. Norell, Gregory M. Erickson, David A. Eberth, Chengkai Jia, and Qi Zhao. "A Basal Tyrannosauroid Dinosaur from the Late Jurassic of China." *Nature* 439 (2006): 715–718.

Zhang, F., Z. Zhou, X. Xu, and X. Wang. "A Juvenile Coelurosaurian Theropod from China Indicates Arboreal Habits." *Naturwissenschaften* 89 (2002): 394–398.

Chapter 4 – The Origin of Birds

Benton, Michael J. *Vertebrate Paleontology*, 3rd ed. Oxford: Blackwell Publishing, 2005.

Carpenter, Kenneth, and Philip J. Currie, eds. *Dinosaur Systematics: Approaches and Perspectives*. Cambridge: Cambridge University Press, 1990.

Colbert, Edwin H. *The Great Dinosaur Hunters and Their Discoveries*. New York: Dover Publications, 1984.

Colbert, Edwin H., and Michael Morales. *Evolution of the Vertebrates*, 4th ed. New York: Wiley-LSS, 1991.

Currie, Philip J., and Kevin Padian, eds. *Encyclopedia of Dinosaurs*. New York: Academic Press, 1997.

Farlow, James O., and Michael K. Brett-Surman, eds. *The Complete Dinosaur*. Bloomington: Indiana University Press, 1999.

Fastovsky, David E., and David B. Weishampel. *The Evolution and Extinction of the Dinosaurs*, 2nd ed. Cambridge: Cambridge University Press, 2005.

Lucas, Spencer G. *Dinosaurs: The Textbook*, 4th ed. New York: McGraw-Hill, 2004.

Norman, David. *Prehistoric Life: The Rise of the Vertebrates*. New York: Macmillan, 1994.

Paul, Gregory S. *Predatory Dinosaurs of the World*. New York: Simon and Schuster, 1988.

———, ed. *The Scientific American Book of Dinosaurs*. New York: St. Martin's Press, 2000.

Prothero, Donald R., and Robert H. Dott Jr. *Evolution of the Earth*. New York: McGraw-Hill, 2004.

Raven, Peter H., George B. Johnson, Jonathan B. Losos, and Susan R. Singer. *Biology*, 7th ed. New York: McGraw-Hill, 2005.

Romer, Alfred S. *Man and the Vertebrates*. Chicago: University of Chicago Press, 1933.

Romer, Alfred S., and Thomas S. Parsons. *The Vertebrate Body, Shorter Version*, 5th ed. Philadelphia: W.B. Saunders, 1978.

Ruben, John A., Terry D. Jones, and Nicholas R. Geist. "Respiratory and Reproductive Paleophysiology of Dinosaurs and Early Birds." *Physiological and Biochemical Zoology* 76 (2003): 141–164.

Schultz, Cesar L., Claiton M.S. Scherer, and Mario C. Barberena. "Biostratigraphy of Southern Brazilian Middle-Upper Triassic." *Revista Brasiliera de Geosciencias* 30, no. 3 (September 2000): 495–498.

Weishampel, David B., Peter Dodson, and Halszka Osmólska, eds. *The Dinosauria*, 2nd ed. Berkeley: University of California Press, 2004.

Chapter 5 – Iguanodontids and Hadrosaurs

Barrett, P.M., R.J. Butler, and F. Knoll. "Small-bodied Ornithischian Dinosaurs from the Middle Jurassic of Sichuan, China." *Journal of Vertebrate Paleontology* 25 (2005): 823–834.

Carpenter, Kenneth, Karl F. Hirsch, and John R. Horner, eds. *Dinosaur Eggs and Babies*. Cambridge: Cambridge University Press, 1994.

Chinsamy, Anusuya. "Ontogenetic Changes in the Bone Histology of the Late Jurassic Ornithopod *Dryosaurus lettowvorbecki*," *Journal of Vertebrate Paleontology* 15 (1995): 96–104.

Ciszek, Debbie. "Asian Elephant." *Animal Diversity Web.* University of Michigan. (September 5, 1997). Available online. URL: http://animaldiversity.ummz.umich.edu/index.html Accessed March 18, 2008.

Evans, D.C., C.A. Forster, and R.R. Reisz. "The Type Specimen of *Tetragonosaurus erectofrons* (Ornithischia: Hadrosauridae) and the Identification of Juvenile Lambeosaurines" In *Dinosaur Provincial Park: a Spectacular Ancient Ecosystem Revealed*, edited by P.J. Currie and E.B. Koppelhus. Bloomington: Indiana University Press, 2005.

Farlow, James O. and Michael K. Brett-Surman, eds. *The Complete Dinosaur.* Bloomington: Indiana University Press, 1997.

Fastovsky, David E., and David B Weishampel. *The Evolution and Extinction of the Dinosaurs.* Cambridge: Cambridge University Press, 1996.

Holmes, Thom. "Singing a Chorus for *Parasaurolophus.*" *Dino Times* 7, no. 7 (July 1997): 1, 3.

———. "All About Hadrosaur Crests." *Dino Times* 7, no. 7 (July 1997): 4–5.

———. "Duckbill Deep Freeze: Early Hadrosaur Discovered in Alaska." *Dino Times* 6, no. 2 (February, 1996): 1–3.

Horner, John R., and James Gorman, *Digging Dinosaurs.* New York: Workman, 1988.

Horner, John R., and Philip J. Currie. "Embryonic and Neonatal Morphology and Ontogeny of a New Species of *Hypacrosaurus* (Ornithischia, Lambeosauridae) from Montana and Alberta." In *Dinosaur Eggs and Babies*, edited by Kenneth Carpenter, Karl F. Hirsch, and John R. Horner. Cambridge: Cambridge University Press, 1994.

Larsson, Hans C.E., Paul C. Sereno, and Jeffrey A. Wilson, "Forebrain Enlargement Among Nonavian Theropod Dinosaurs," *Journal of Vertebrate Paleontology* 20, no. 3 (September 2000): 615–618.

Molnar, R.E. "Observations on the Australian Ornithopod Dinosaur, *Muttaburrasaurus.*" *Memoirs of the Queensland Museum* 39 (1996): 639–652.

Moratalla, J.J., and J.E. Powell. "Dinosaur Nesting Patterns." In *Dinosaur Eggs and Babies*, edited by Kenneth Carpenter, Karl F. Hirsch, and John R. Horner. Cambridge: Cambridge University Press, 1994.

Russell, Dale A. *An Odyssey in Time.* Toronto: University of Toronto Press, 1989.

Sues, Hans-Dieter, and David B. Norman. "Hypsilophodontidae, *Tenontosaurus*, Dryosauridae." In *The Dinosauria*, edited by David B. Weishampel, Peter Dodson, and Halszka Osmólska. Berkeley: University of California Press, 1990.

Tiffney, Bruce H. "Land Plants as Food and Habitat in the Age of Dinosaurs." In *The Complete Dinosaur*, edited by James O. Farlow and Michael K. Brett-Surman. *The Complete Dinosaur.* Bloomington: Indiana University Press, 1997.

Varricchio, David J. "Growth and Embryology." In *The Encyclopedia of Dinosaurs,* edited by Philip J. Currie and Kevin Padian. New York: Academic Press, 1997.

Wallace, Joseph. *The American Museum of Natural History's Book of Dinosaurs and Other Ancient Creatures.* New York: Simon and Schuster, 1994.

Weishampel, David, and John R. Horner, "Life History Syndromes, Heterochrony, and the Evolution of Dinosaurs." In *Dinosaur Eggs and Babies,* edited by Kenneth Carpenter, Karl F. Hirsch, and John R. Horner. Cambridge: Cambridge University Press, 1994.

Weishampel, David B., and Lawrence M. Witmer. "Heterodontosauridae." In *The Dinosauria,* edited by David B. Weishampel, Peter Dodson, and Halszka Osmólska. Berkeley: University of California Press, 1990.

Winkler, D.A., P.A. Murry, and L.L. Jacobs. "A New Species of *Tenontosaurus* (Dinosauria: Ornithopoda) from the Early Cretaceous of Texas." *Journal of Vertebrate Paleontology* 17 (1997): 330–348.

Chapter 6 – Horned and Bone-Headed Dinosaurs

Benton, Michael J. "Origin and Interrelationships of Dinosaurs." In *The Dinosauria*, edited by David B. Weishampel, Peter Dodson, and Halszka Osmólska. Berkeley: University of California Press, 1990.

Sereno, Paul. "The Evolution of Dinosaurs." *Science* 284 (June 25, 1999): 2137.

Xu, X., C.A. Forster, J.M. Clark, and J. Mo. "A Basal Ceratopsian with Transitional Features from the Late Jurassic of Northwestern China." *Proceedings of the Royal Society of London* B 273 (2006): 2135–2140.

Zhao, X., Z. Cheng, and X. Xu. "The Earliest Ceratopsian from the Tuchengzi Formation of Liaoning, China." *Journal of Vertebrate Paleontology* 19 (1999): 681–691.

Zhao, X., Z. Cheng, X. Xu, and P.J. Makovicky. "A New Ceratopsian from the Upper Jurassic Houcheng Formation of Hebei, China." *Acta Geologica Sinica (English Edition)* 80 (2006): 467–473.

Chapter 7 – Pterosaurs: Flying Reptiles of the Mesozoic Era

Bramwell, Cherrie. "The First Hot-Blooded Flappers," *Spektrum* 69 (1970): 12–14.

Currie, Philip J., and Kevin Padian, eds. *The Encyclopedia of Dinosaurs.* New York: Academic Press, 1997.

Dodson, Peter. "Quantitative Aspects of Relative Growth and Sexual Dimorphism in *Protoceratops*," *Journal of Paleontology* 50 (September 1976): 929–940.

Edinger, Tilly. "Das Gehirn der Pterosaurier," *Zeitschrift für Anatomie und Entwicklungsgeschichte* 82, nos. 1/3 (1927): 105–112.

Lockley, Martin, and Adrian P. Hunt. *Dinosaur Tracks and other Fossil Footprints of the Western United States.* New York: Columbia University Press, 1995.

Seeley, Harry Govier. "On the Pterodactyle as Evidence of a New Subclass of Vertebrates (Saurornia)." *Reports of the British Association for the Advancement of Science* 34 (1864): 69.

Sharov, A.G. "New Flying Reptiles from the Mesozoic of Kazakhstan and Kirgizia." *Akademia Nauk, Paleontological Institute*, no. 130 (1971): 104–113.

Steiler, Carl, "Neur Rekonstruktionsversuch eines Liassichen Flugsauriers," *Naturwissenschaftliche Wochenschrift*, 21, no. 20 (1922): 273–280.

Unwin, David M. "Variable Growth Rate and Delayed Maturation: Do They Explain 'Giant' Pterosaurs?" *Journal of Vertebrate Paleontology, Abstracts of Papers* 21, supplement to no. 3 (August 22, 2001): 109–110.

Unwin, David M., and Natasha N. Bakhurina, "*Sordes pilosus* and the Nature of the Pterosaur Flight Apparatus," *Nature* 371 (1994): 62–64.

Wellnhofer, Peter. *The Illustrated Encyclopedia of Pterosaurs.* New York, Crescent Books, 1991.

———. "Die Rhamphorhynchoidea (Pterosauria) der Oberjura-Plattenkalke Süddeutschlands Teil III: Palökologie und Stammersgeschichte." *Palaeontographica* (A), no. 149 (1975): 1–30.

Wharton, Deborah S. "The Evolution of the Avian Brain." *Journal of Vertebrate Paleontology, Abstracts of Papers* 21, supplement to no. 3 (August 22, 2001): 113.

Chapter 8 – Marine Reptiles of the Mesozoic Era

Augusta, Josef. *Prehistoric Sea Monsters*. London: Paul Hamlyn, 1964.

Bell, Gordon L., M.A. Sheldon, J.P. Lamb, and J.E. Martin, "The First Evidence of Live Birth in Mosasauridae (Squamata): Exceptional Preservation in the Cretaceous Pierre Shale of South Dakota." *Journal of Vertebrate Paleontology* 16 (suppl. no. 3) (1996): 21A–22A.

Benton, Michael J. "Origin and Interrelationships of Dinosaurs." In *The Dinosauria*, edited by David B. Weishampel, Peter Dodson, and Halszka Osmólska. Berkeley: University of California Press, 1990.

Callaway, Jack M., and Elizabeth L. Nicholls, eds. *Ancient Marine Reptiles*. San Diego: Academic Press, 1997.

Cheng, Y.-N., X.-C. Wu, and Q. Ji. "Triassic Marine Reptiles Gave Birth to Live Young." *Nature* 432 (2004): 383–386.

Conybeare, W.D. "Additional Notices on the Fossil Genera *Ichthyosaurus* and *Plesiosaurus*." *Transactions of the Geological Society of London* 2, no. 1 (1822): 103–123.

Dalla Vecchia, F.M. "A New Sauropterygian Reptile with Plesiosaurian Affinity from the Late Triassic of Italy." *Rivista Italiana di Paleontologia e Stratigrafia* 112 (2006): 207–225.

Everhart, Mike. "Gastroliths Associated with Plesiosaur Remains in the Sharon Springs Member of the Pierre Shale (Late Cretaceous), Western Kansas." *Transactions of the Kansas Academy of Science* 103 no. 1–2 (2000): 58–69.

Forrest, R. "A possible Early Elasmosaurian Plesiosaur from the Triassic/Jurassic Boundary of Nottinghamshire." *Mercian Geologist* 14 (1998): 135–143.

Haines, Tim. *Walking With Dinosaurs*. New York: Dorling Kindersley, 1999.

Kauffman, E.G., and R.V. Kesling. "An Upper Cretaceous Ammonite Bitten by a Mosasaur." *Contributions from the Museum of Paleontology, University of Michigan* 15, no. 9 (1960): 193–248.

Lee, Michael S.Y., John D. Scanlon, and Michael W. Caldwell, "Snake Origins." *Science* 288 (2000): 343–1344.

Lingham-Soliar, Theagarten. "Plesiosaur Locomotion: Is the Four-Wing Problem Real or Merely an Atheoretical Exercise?" *Neues Jahrbuch für Geologie und Paläontologie, Abhandlungen* 217 (2000): 45–87.

———. "What Happened 65 Million Years Ago?" *Science Spectra* 17 (1999): 20–29.

Martill, Dave, and Darren Naish. *Walking With Dinosaurs: The Evidence.* New York: Dorling Kindersley, 2000.

Martin, Larry D., and Bruce M. Rothschild. "Paleopathology and Diving Mosasaurs." *American Scientist* 77 (1989): 460–467.

Motani, Ryosuke. "Rulers of the Jurassic Seas." *Scientific American* (December 2000). Available online. URL: http://www.sciam.com/article.cfm?id=rulers-of-the-jurassic-se. Accessed May 29, 2008.

Naish, Darren. "Diet of *Liopleurodon.*" *Archives of the Dinosaur Mailing List.* (November 12, 1996). Available online. URL: http://dml.cmnh.org/1966Nov/msg00296.html. Accessed May 29, 2008.

———. "Placodonts: The Bizarre 'Walrus-Turtles' of the Triassic." *Oceans of Kansas* Web site, http://www.oceansofkansas.com/placodnt.html (updated March 26, 2004). Accessed March 24, 2008.

Rieppel, O. "*Paraplacodus* and ther phylogeny of the Placodontia (Reptilia: Sauropterygia)." *Zoological Journal of the Linnean Society* 130 (2000): 635–659.

Robinson, Jane A. "The Locomotion of Plesiosaurs." *Neues Jahrbuch für Geologie und Paläontologie*, Abhandlungen 153 (1975): 86–128.

Sato, Tsutomu, and Kazushige Tanabe. "Cretaceous Plesiosaurs ate Ammonites." *Nature* 394 (August 13, 1998): 629–630.

Scotese, Christopher R. *Paleomap Project.* November 19, 2001. Available online. URL: www.scotese.com. Accessed March 24, 2008.

Sereno, Paul, "The Evolution of Dinosaurs." *Science* 284 (June 25, 1999): 2137.

Storrs, Glenn. "Fossil Vertebrate Faunas of the British Rhaetian (latest Triassic)." *Zoological Journal of the Linnaean Society* 112 (1994): 217–259.

Conclusion

Lingham-Soliar, Theagarten. "What Happened 65 Million Years Ago?" *Science Spectra* 17 (1999): 20–29.

David M. Raup. *Extinction: Bad Genes or Bad Luck?* New York, W.W. Norton, 1991.

FURTHER READING

Benton, Michael J. *Vertebrate Paleontology*, 3rd ed. Oxford: Blackwell Publishing, 2005.

Carpenter, Kenneth. *Eggs, Nests, and Baby Dinosaurs: A New Look at Dinosaur Reproduction*. Bloomington: Indiana University Press, 1999.

Carpenter, Kenneth, and Philip J. Currie, eds. *Dinosaur Systematics: Approaches and Perspectives*. Cambridge: Cambridge University Press, 1990.

Carpenter, Kenneth, Karl F. Hirsch, and John R. Horner, eds. *Dinosaur Eggs and Babies*. Cambridge: Cambridge University Press, 1994.

Charig, Alan J. *A New Look at the Dinosaurs*. New York: Facts on File, 1983.

Colbert, Edwin H. *The Great Dinosaur Hunters and Their Discoveries*. New York: Dover Publications, 1984.

Colbert, Edwin H., and Michael Morales. *Evolution of the Vertebrates*, 4th ed. New York: Wiley-LSS, 1991.

Currie, Philip J., and Kevin Padian, eds. *Encyclopedia of Dinosaurs*. New York: Academic Press, 1997.

Ellis, Richard. *No Turning Back: The Life and Death of Animal Species*. New York: Harper Collins, 2004.

Farlow, James O., and Michael K. Brett-Surman, eds. *The Complete Dinosaur*. Bloomington: Indiana University Press, 1999.

Fastovsky, David E., and David B. Weishampel. *The Evolution and Extinction of the Dinosaurs*, 2nd ed. Cambridge: Cambridge University Press, 2005.

Fortey, Richard. *Life: A Natural History of the First Four Billion Years of Life on Earth*. New York: Alfred A. Knopf, 1998.

Gould, Stephen Jay, ed. *The Book of Life*. New York: W.W. Norton, 1993.

Holmes, Thom. *Fossil Feud: The Rivalry of the First American Dinosaur Hunters*. Parsippany, N.J.: Julian Messner, 1998.

———. *Great Dinosaur Expeditions and Discoveries: Adventures with the Fossil Hunters*. Berkeley Heights, N.J.: Enslow Publishers, 2003.

————. *Prehistoric Flying Reptiles: The Pterosaurs.* Berkeley Heights, N.J.: Enslow Publishers, 2003.

Lambert, David. *Encyclopedia of Prehistory.* New York: Facts on File, 2002.

Lucas, Spencer G. *Chinese Fossil Vertebrates.* New York: Columbia University Press, 2001.

————. *Dinosaurs: The Textbook,* 4th ed. New York: McGraw-Hill, 2004.

Margulis, Lynn, and Karlene V. Schwartz. *Five Kingdoms: An Illustrated Guide to the Phyla of Life on Earth,* 3rd ed. New York: W.H. Freeman, 1998.

Norman, David B. *Prehistoric Life: The Rise of the Vertebrates.* New York: Macmillan, 1994.

Norell, Mark A. *Unearthing the Dragon: The Great Feathered Dinosaur Discovery.* New York: Pi Press, 2005.

Palmer, Douglas. *Atlas of the Prehistoric World.* New York: Discovery Books, 1999.

Paul, Gregory S. *Predatory Dinosaurs of the World.* New York: Simon and Schuster, 1988.

Paul, Gregory S., ed. *The Scientific American Book of Dinosaurs.* New York: St. Martin's Press, 2000.

Prothero, Donald R., and Robert H. Dott Jr. *Evolution of the Earth.* New York: McGraw-Hill, 2004.

Raven, Peter H., George B. Johnson, Jonathan B. Losos, and Susan R. Singer. *Biology,* 7th ed. New York: McGraw-Hill, 2005.

Unwin, David. *The Pterosaurs from Deep Time.* New York: Pi Press, 2006.

Weishampel, David B., Peter Dodson, and Halszka Osmólska, eds. *The Dinosauria,* 2nd ed. Berkeley: University of California Press, 2004.

Wellnhofer, Peter. *The Illustrated Encyclopedia of Pterosaurs.* New York: Crescent Books, 1991.

Internet Sites

American Museum of Natural History. Vertebrate Evolution

An interactive diagram of vertebrate evolution with links to example fossil specimens in the world-famous collection of this museum.

http://www.amnh.org/exhibitions/permanent/fossilhalls/ vertebrate/

Australian Museum. Palaeontology

An extensive visual guide to Australian fossils.

http://www.austmus.gov.au/palaeontology/index.htm

Bernard Price Institute For Palaeontological Research, University of the Witwatersrand, Johannesburg. Fossil Picture Gallery

Information for a wide variety of South African vertebrate fossils.

http://www.wits.ac.za/geosciences/bpi/fossilpictures.htm

Carnegie Museum of Natural History. Dinosaurs in Their Time Exhibit

A guide to the exhibits and specimens of the recently updated dinosaur halls of the Carnegie Museum of Natural History, keeper of many important North American dinosaur specimens.

http://www.carnegiemnh.org/dinosaurs/index.htm

Creisler, Ben. Dinosaur Translation and Pronunciation Guide

This excellent Web site not only provides a pronunciation guide to the names of dinosaurs, but also offers some historical background on many of the names and specimens that broadens one's understanding of their discovery and significance.

http://www.dinosauria.com/dml/names/dinoa.htm

International Commission on Stratigraphy. International Stratigraphic Chart

Downloadable geologic time scales provided by the International Commission on Stratigraphy.

http://www.stratigraphy.org/cheu.pdf

Lapworth Museum, University of Birmingham. Palaeontological Collections: Vertebrate Collection

Online exhibit exploring early vertebrate life from the United Kingdom.

http://www.lapworth.bham.ac.uk/collections/palaeontology/vertebrates.htm

Kazlev, Alan, and Augustus White. Palaeos: The Trace of Life on Earth

A robust and growing reference about all kinds of life-forms.

http://www.palaeos.com/

Maddison, D.R., and K.-S. Schulz. The Tree of Life Web Project

The Tree of Life Web Project is a meticulously designed view of life-forms based on their phylogenetic (evolutionary) connections. It is hosted by the University of Arizona College of Agriculture and Life Sciences and the University of Arizona Library.

http://tolweb.org/tree/phylogeny.html

Paleontology Portal. Vertebrates

A resource exploring early vertebrate life, produced by the University of California Museum of Paleontology, the Paleontological Society, the Society of Vertebrate Paleontology, and the United States Geological Survey.

http://www.paleoportal.org/index.php?globalnav=fossil_gallery &sectionnav=taxon&taxon_id=16

Public Broadcasting Service. Evolution Library: Evidence for Evolution

This resource outlines the extensive evidence in support of both the fact and theory of evolution, basing its approach on studies of the fossil record, molecular sequences, and comparative anatomy.

http://www.pbs.org/wgbh/evolution/library/04/

Scotese, Christopher R. Paleomap Project

A valuable source of continental maps showing the positioning of Earth's continents over the course of geologic time.

http://www.scotese.com/

University of California Museum of Paleontology. Fossil Evidence: Transitional Forms

A tutorial about transitional forms in the fossil record, with illustrated examples.

http://evolution.berkeley.edu/evosite/lines/IAtransitional.shtml.

Virtual Fossil Museum. Fossils Across Geological Time and Evolution

A privately funded, image-rich educational resource dedicated to fossils. Contributors include amateur and professional paleontologists.

http://www.fossilmuseum.net/index.htm

Picture Credits

INDEX

ABOUT THE AUTHOR

THOM HOLMES is a writer specializing in natural history subjects and dinosaurs. He is noted for his expertise on the early history of dinosaur science in America. He was the publications director of *The Dinosaur Society* for six years (1991–1997) and the editor of its newsletter, *Dino Times*, the world's only monthly publication devoted to news about dinosaur discoveries. It was through the Society and his work with the Academy of Natural Sciences in Philadelphia that Thom developed widespread contacts and working relationships with paleontologists and paleo-artists throughout the world.

Thom's published works include *Fossil Feud: The Rivalry of America's First Dinosaur Hunters* (Silver Burdett Press, September 1997); *The Dinosaur Library* (Enslow, 2001–2002); *Duel of the Dinosaur Hunters* (Pearson Education, 2002); and *Fossil Feud: The First American Dinosaur Hunters* (Silver Burdett/Julian Messner, 1997). His many honors and awards include the National Science Teachers Association's *Outstanding Science Book of 1998,* VOYA's 1997 Nonfiction Honor List, an Orbis Pictus Honor, and the Chicago Public Library Association's *"Best of the Best"* in science books for young people.

Thom did undergraduate work in geology and studied paleontology through his role as a staff educator with the Academy of Natural Sciences in Philadelphia. He is a regular participant in field exploration, with two recent expeditions to Patagonia in association with Canadian, American, and Argentinian universities.